T0082408

Endorsements for
Who Told You That?

"Pastor Neill's biblical insight, top-shelf storytelling, integrity with the word of God, and honesty about the human condition make *Who Told You That?* a must-read. If you want to refresh, renew, and rebuild your faith, spend time right here in this fantastic book. Prepare to be blessed!"

—Rev. Corey Bjertness,
Ret. Senior Pastor, First Lutheran Church

"*Who Told You That?* equips readers to confront the cultural lies that too often distort perceptions of self and society to stand in the way of a peace-filled life. With a delicate pastoral touch, Neill draws on the power of Scripture and story to discover truth from lies in life's moments of struggle, doubt, and heartbreak, as well as those of forgiveness, hope, and joy. Each chapter provides a lively springboard for inspiring group discussion or personal reflection, encouraging readers to ground their thoughts and actions in timeless truths."

—Marianna Malm, educator

"*Who Told You That?* is a well-written and important book. The author uses humor and personal stories to connect with the audience and address the larger issues that most of us struggle with. The topic of recognizing lies and the debilitating effect they have on our lives is thoroughly dealt with. Each chapter makes a case supported by logic and backed by Bible references. The 'Thoughts to Consider' study questions make the content immediately applicable to daily life. This is a book that has practical implications for personal and spiritual growth, and that makes it worth reading."

—Montana Lattin,
Theater Arts Coordinator / Rosie International / Middle East

"The precious words by the Father which are the basis of this helpful book have been the foundation of my self-esteem over many years. Thank you for such a complete, honest, and compelling study of the text."

—Rev. Matthew O. Valan

Comments from participants
of a study using *Who Told You That?*

"The study was excellent. I have benefitted so much from it. Everything is clear and easy to understand. I especially like the way the 'lies' and 'truths' were spelled out clearly and can be referred to easily, which I will be doing frequently! I learned that everyone has bad feelings about themselves—I thought it was just me. Freeing!"

—*Judy Hanawalt*

"I appreciated the biblical foundation of your material as well as the integration of lecture and discussion/personal sharing."

—*Peter Schmidt*

"I appreciated you including your personal experiences relating to each topic. I learned how easy it is to fall into the trap of believing mistruths we tell ourselves or are reinforced from others."

—*Renee Radloff*

"I struggled with 'believing the lie.' This study explained to me what I have been doing. It was very clear and easy to understand. It was a surprise to learn that I've been listening to Satan."

—*Mary Ann Phillips*

who told you that?

BY
LAURIE ETTA NEILL

Published by Deep River Books
Sisters, Oregon
www.deepriverbooks.com

Cover design by Laurie Etta Neill and Jennifer Klath

ISBN—13: 9781632695857
Library of Congress Control Number: 2022916477

Printed in the USA
2022—First Edition
31 30 29 28 27 26 25 24 23 22   10 9 8 7 6 5 4 3 2 1

Table of Contents

Prologue

*"Then you will know the truth, and the truth
will set you free"*

(John 8:32 NIV).

When I was eleven years old, the rock opera *Jesus Christ Superstar* took the teen scene by storm. My older sisters were really into it. (Could it have been the lead actor Ted Neeley's chiseled chin and long hair?) My parents, on the other hand, were not so sure this rock opera was safe. Was it blasphemous? Were they risking their children's everlasting souls by allowing them to play the record over and over again?

I have my own love affair with this album and know every word to every song by heart. (But it has to be the 1970 original concept album with British rock stars Murray Head and Ian Gillan. Yes, I am that picky.)

The premise of this book is that the truthful answer to the question, "Who told you that?" has the power to change lives. This quest for a truthful response requires an exploration of what truth is. The first thought that runs through my mind comes from lyrics from *Jesus Christ Superstar.* While being questioned by Pontius

Pilate, Jesus says, "I look for truth and find that I get damned," to which Pilate replies, "What is truth? Is truth unchanging law? We both have truths. Are mine the same as yours?"

What is truth? Is it the same as a fact? Is truth relative or absolute? We swear to tell the truth, the whole truth, and nothing but the truth. Does that mean there are unspoken truths, half-truths, or variances of the truth? Are there "alternative facts"? Is what I consider true for myself also true for you? For example, I cannot prove that God exists, yet I have dedicated my life's work to the belief that he does. On the other hand, I cannot prove God does not exist. Neither can you.

The truth matters. What we believe about God and about ourselves determines our emotional and spiritual well-being. The tenet of Scripture is that God is truth, Satan is the lie. The truth is transformational and liberating. The lie is darkness and death. For too many years, I allowed faulty beliefs to steal my peace and negatively affect my emotional well-being. Identifying lies and replacing them with the truth of God's Word changed my life. My desire is to help God's Word do the same for you.

Scripture is clear that every utterance from the Lord possesses the quality of truth. Truth is a fundamental characteristic and virtue of God. God's truth is not only absolute; it is a person. Jesus says he is the truth and promises his ministry of the truth will continue when the Spirit of truth comes after him (John 14:6, 16–17). The apostle Paul and others repeatedly make the point that those who are void of the truth are entangled in darkness because they have bought into the lies of the world.

The lie is diametrically opposed to the truth and personified by Satan. Jesus admonished some Jews gathered around him, saying, "You are of your father the devil and your will is to do your father's desires. He was a murderer from the beginning and does not stand in the truth, because there is no truth in him. When he lies, he speaks out of his character, for he is a liar and the father of lies" (John 8:44). The father of lies wants us to believe that God is not who he says he is and that we are not who God says we are. That is the quicksand that catches us and slowly pulls us under. It is the slippery foundation of all our problems and misbehaviors.

My hope in writing this book is to offer practical steps to recognize the lies of the world and to learn how to battle them with the truth of God. I present formulas, stories, and Scripture—effective and practical tools in the battle against misbeliefs. You will be introduced to a step-by-step formula—The Lie Detector—that has the power to change your life. We will flush out this formula in chapter 5.

However, I am not interested in writing a self-help book. If this book is not about Christ and what he can do, has done, and will do for you, it is not worthy of your time. If these writings are only about your efforts, then this endeavor becomes a book full of good advice.

It is Christ who transforms. True freedom comes from a relationship with him. Beware of any formula that causes or allows you to take your focus off the person of Christ. Jesus said, "And I, when I am lifted up from the earth, will draw all people to myself" (John 12:32). My prayer is that the words written here will lift up Christ alone so that he may draw you to him, and in meeting him, you become a new and free creation (2 Corinthians 5:17).

In his devotional book, *My Utmost for His Highest*, evangelist Oswald Chambers repeatedly reminds us that our focus is not to be on doctrine, works, beliefs, or causes: "There is only one relationship that really matters and that is your personal relationship to your personal Redeemer and Lord. If you maintain that at all costs, letting everything else go, God will fulfill his purpose through your life."[1]

Replacing the lie with the truth will pave the way for the fruit of the Spirit of truth to manifest in your life. The fruit of the Spirit includes love, joy, peace, patience, kindness, generosity, faithfulness, gentleness, and self-control (Galatians 5:22–23). All of these can be yours, today.

Living a life based on the truth may not change our circumstances, but it will change *us*. We may not be delivered from adversity, but we will be able to navigate adversity with peace and emotional well-being. God will give us himself, and ultimately that is what we need.

"Seek first his kingdom and his righteousness, and all these things will be given to you" (Matthew 6:33 NIV).

In Truth,
Laurie Etta Neill

PART 1

⚡

The Truth vs. The Lie

CHAPTER 1

"And [God] said, 'Who told you that you were naked?'"

(Genesis 3:11 NIV).

I grew up on a ranch in Montana, four miles from a sleepy little town along the Missouri River. It was an amazing place to be a child. The Teton River was a short walk away, and in the summer heat my siblings and I practically lived between its muddy banks. Some of my fondest memories are the lazy days we floated the river between the Carter and Green Roof Bridges, the latter being a short walk back to the house—or a quick run if the horseflies were chasing you.

Dilapidated cabins dotted the landscape, silently rotting away among the tumbleweeds. If they had stories to tell of the settlers who occupied them, they were hidden behind the worm-eaten walls.

A narrow, washboard road stood between us and town. The road meandered its way up a hill steep enough to sled down in the winter, and neglected enough to keep us home when snow and ice became too hazardous. We walked up that hill in the morning to meet the school bus and ran down that hill in the afternoon to find a snack waiting on the kitchen table.

Good times.

But it was isolating. I spent many hours sitting at the kitchen table, gazing up the hill and hoping to see a car drive down the winding road. Not many visitors ventured our way, and I was rarely exposed to anyone outside of my family. It may be a surprise to those who know me now, but I was painfully shy growing up. If someone came to the door, I hid behind my mother's legs with my arms wrapped around her knees and my face buried in her sweater. My lack of socialization alarmed her enough to pay a lady in town, Mrs. Hanson, to watch me during the day.

Mrs. Hanson's husband, a brutal man with dark clouds in his eyes, was especially mean to the foster children they were raising. Instead of becoming "socialized," I became scared of being noticed. I did not want to experience the brunt of his anger. He believed children were to be seen and not heard. So, I lived a low-key existence.

It was there that I had some of my first lessons on the unfairness of life. One Easter, we were served eggs for lunch, but Mrs. Hanson burned the edges of the eggs. I did not want to eat them, but if I didn't, I would not be allowed a chocolate bunny for dessert. Of course, I would almost do anything for chocolate, so I gagged down the eggs—only to throw them up again. Because I had thrown up, I was forced to lie on the couch the rest of the afternoon while I watched everyone else enjoy the special dessert and go on an egg hunt. To this day, I can only eat eggs if they are barely cooked.

The church we attended was a lifesaver in one way and a soul-crusher in another. I finally started coming out of my shell as I became acquainted with other children in Sunday School. I gained some confidence, always being cast as Mary in the Christmas play and experiencing the honor of being an acolyte during worship. I went on sledding parties and helped my mom with art projects for Vacation Bible School.

The one thing I was not exposed to, though, was grace. This denomination was law-driven and doled out shame quickly and abundantly. The message, as I received it, was: if you wanted any kind of favor, you had to earn it. This experience, paired with my experience with Mrs. Hanson's husband, made me believe that my worth was attached to my behavior and that if I made a mistake, I had no one to blame but myself and I should be ashamed.

Evidence of this belief is my issue with the movie *Willy Wonka and the Chocolate Factory.* Charlie and his Grandpa Joe, toward the end of the factory tour, drink Fizzy Lifting Drink and become filled with gas. They float to the top of the room like balloons. Eventually, they are in danger of being sucked into the ceiling's spinning fan. Before disaster strikes, they discover they can burp their way down to safety.

After the tour, Willy Wonka was furious at the two for stealing the off-limits Fizzy Lifting Drinks and told them they had lost the lifetime supply of chocolate prize for violating the contract. As Charlie and his grandpa turn to leave, Charlie returns the Everlasting Gobstopper candy that Wonka had given him earlier in the tour. Wonka's face lights up in delight as he declares Charlie has passed the test by not keeping the Gobstopper and selling it to Wonka's competitor, Mr. Slugworth. He declares Charlie the winner!

But how can that be? He broke the rules! Because he stole the Fizzy Lifting Drink and touched the ceiling; the dutiful Oompa Loompas had to wash and sterilize it. Charlie should be ashamed of himself, yet he hardly showed any remorse when his wrongdoing was exposed. This, my friends, has always bothered me.

I know it makes me sound like a heartless fool, but that is the type of action that causes my fairness needle to spike off the chart.

The belief that worth and behavior were inextricably linked made me a very good student, a well-behaved teen, and earned me the "goody two-shoes" moniker in high school. Everyone knew if you needed something done, give it to Laurie, the Reliable One.

I had other nicknames as well. I was tall and lanky, so my basketball mates nicknamed me "Ligaments." I was not the brightest in math, so Bart (whom I had a crush on, so it was doubly painful) nicknamed me "Meat-head Etta." My siblings had a much stricter upbringing than I did, so they called me "spoiled brat," which was true. I stumbled upon a gathering in my brother's bedroom and was told to go away because they were having a "Hate Laurie Club" meeting—and my brother was the president.

As I look back on these labels, they are not so awfully painful anymore, but I see how they allowed negative and false beliefs about my worth to put a footprint in the wet cement of my psyche.

Nicknames and labels given through life often stick with us. Sometimes names are a term of endearment, but other labels grow out of our pain. These harmful messages plant falsehoods that become tangled up with who we believe we are. A friend of mine says her dad's nickname for her was "stupid." Even though she recognizes that his insecurity was a contributor to his name-calling, it still hurt. If we hear something enough times, the wet cement dries and our identity is forever linked to another person's—or society's—opinion of us. Our worth becomes linked to our weight, intelligence, relationships, social status, health—and the list goes on.

In an attempt to fit in, my friend Mark, on his first day of high school, ate a fly. Other boys from chemistry class dared him to, so he did, not wanting to appear intimidated. For the rest of his high school career, he was ridiculed with the nickname "Fly."

What part of your true self have you sacrificed to fit in? What aspect of your looks, personality, intelligence, or experiences has ended up being your "fly?"

Throughout my life, I allowed the cement of my identity to have imprints that were not true. I believed I was what I accomplished, how I appeared, what I acquired, what I felt, and whatever other people said I was.

But the most devastating and deepest imprint came in my adult years when I went through my divorce—and that footprint impressed upon me beliefs that I was unlovable and a complete failure. I was rejected and abandoned by the one who swore to love me for better or worse. Whether it was true or not, I felt he did not think I was worth the effort.

During those dark days, someone gave me a "Dammit Doll." You were to take it by its long legs and hit its head on the table, and yell, "Damn it," as you took out your frustrations. I was steeped in self-pity, so slamming something's head into a table seemed a promising way to release the pent-up tornado that was whirling inside me. I took the doll and repeatedly hit it on the kitchen table, yelling "Damn it!" repeatedly. I was raised to never cuss, so this curse in and of itself was a big step for me. Unfortunately, my aim was off, and I hit my knuckle on the tabletop, which immediately swelled up, leaving me in pain for weeks. That is how much of a failure I was—I could not even wallow correctly. Perhaps it was punishment for swearing.

But as he is known to do, God worked good from something devastating. I remember seeking out others who had gone through what I was currently experiencing and asking them how they survived, because I could not see a way out. The shame of failing and the guilt of raising my two young sons in a broken home (I hate that term) smothered me like a heavy old coat. Fortunately, I remembered from growing up in the church that there was a God who loved me, even if I felt I was not worth it. I had not been in touch with God for a long time, but I knew deep in my heart that his love was still true. So, I went back to church. My pain drove me back to a God who welcomed me with open arms. And slowly, he began to soften the cement of my psyche and level out the imprints I had allowed to take hold. I still had many questions for him—but God and I took it one step at a time.

During this time, one question became a lifesaver for me. It is the question that God asks of Adam and Eve. They had believed the lie of Satan over the truth of God and had eaten the forbidden fruit. Immediately they realized they were naked, even though they had been naked all along (Gen. 2:25). Their clothing had been innocence, light, love, and grace. They were image-bearers of their Creator. Now they were clothed in shame and fear. I could relate.

We too were created to be clothed in light, love, and grace, but we have believed lies about who God is and who we are. And those lies have left us feeling naked and exposed.

God called to Adam and Eve and wondered where they were, although he knew perfectly well. Adam answered God, "I was afraid because I was naked; so I hid." God said, "Who told you that you were naked?" (Gen. 3:10–11).

Who told you that? That was God's question for Adam and Eve, and it is his question for us. We clad ourselves with labels and nicknames instead of believing we are the apple of God's eye. At that time, I was sure I was a failure, unlovable, stupid, and worthless. God asked me, point-blank: "Who told you that?"

It certainly was not God. He tells me just the opposite. The Bible is a love story between a Creator and his creation. It is a story about the great lengths God went to in order to show me how loved and worthy I am. Incredibly treasured. Incredibly valued. But the truth of that had been masked by the lies the world offered up and I grabbed onto.

What do you believe about yourself? Maybe it is, "I'm stupid." Who told you that? "I have no purpose." Who told you that? "I am a failure. I cannot do anything right." Who told you that? Your boss? Your spouse? Your parents? A teacher? Your illness? Your own self-talk?

Once I was offering a Bible study at church that was to start on a Tuesday, September 29. That was the date I advertised in one publication, but in another publication, I advertised the start date as September 19, which was not even a Tuesday. I did not catch my error until it was printed in an advertisement in 25,000 magazines distributed throughout the community. Then I noticed in the ad in a bulletin, and on a website, I had indicated the start date as September 15. One study—three different start dates. What could go wrong with that?

A couple days later, I sent out a thousand postcards asking people to "sing" [sic] up for a "marraige" [sic] retreat.

Sigh.

When I realized my mistakes, I thought, "Oh Laurie, how can you be so stupid?" The ironic twist is that the women's study was about combating negative self-talk.

I would never tell others they were stupid, yet I allow myself to say it to myself often. And guessing by the number of women who came to the study, many others struggle with this affliction as well. We speak grace to others, so let us speak grace to ourselves. Once I realized my three-dates fiasco, I said, "Well God, you're bigger than my mistakes, and it will be OK."

When your own voice, or voices from your past or present, echo messages that belittle your worth, try this instead:

"I am lovable." Who told you that? God did (Col. 3:12).

"I am accepted." Who told you that? God did (Rom. 15:7; John 6:37).

"I am free." Who told you that? God did (Gal. 5:1).

"I am forgiven." Who told you that? God did (Eph. 1:7).

"I am bold, confident, and welcomed into God's presence." Who told you that? God did (Eph. 3:12).

God invites you to examine any message that does not jibe with his truth, recognize it as filth, and toss it out. Get rid of anything you believe about yourself that is incongruent with what God says about you. Run your self-talk through the filter of God's Word. That practice is the only way to begin to recognize the lies that have hijacked your identity and replace them with the truth. (We will gain tools on how to do that for the remainder of our time together.)

I will continue to try hard to live error-free, and I know I will fail. In the book of James, we are told, "For all of us make many mistakes" (James 3:2). Ain't that the truth! But those mistakes do not define us.

"Who told you that?" The idea that a mere question can change your life sounds easy. It is—and it is not. Labels go deep. Tapes of negative messages are hard to erase. Solid cement is difficult to break apart. But it is worth the effort to reject the lies that strip us of the garments of glory and robes of righteousness we are meant to don (Isa. 61:10). Free yourself from the bondage of negative labels by knowing the truth of God, which sets you free (John 8:32).

Knowing the truth begins by knowing the enemy and his weapons of deceit. And make no mistake about it, this is war. Are you ready? Let's go!

For Personal or Group Study:

Thoughts to Consider

- At what age did you realize life was unfair?
- What brought you to that realization?
- Were you raised in a shame-based household, church, or school?
- What spikes your fairness needle off the charts?
- What part of yourself have you sacrificed in order to fit in?
- What lies have you believed about yourself, and who told them to you?
- What experiences have left you feeling unlovable?
- What are your earliest memories of the church and of God?

Detect the Lie

- You should be ashamed of yourself.
- Your worth is attached to your behavior.
- You can earn favor with God if you are a "goodie two-shoes."
- Your given labels and nicknames are a reflection of who you are.

- Your ability to "fit in" goes a long way in determining your quality of life.
- You have been away from God for so long that he might not want you back.

Argue against the Lie

- Shame has no place in God's kingdom.
- Worth is determined by your Creator and no one else.
- Labels and nicknames do not define you.
- God's opinion of you is the only one that ultimately matters.
- God's Word is a lie-filter.
- You can have emotional and spiritual health and wholeness when you root yourself in God's truth, which is God's Word.

Replace the Lie with the Truth (God's Word)

- "The sum of your [God's] word is truth" (Ps. 119:160).
- "But God told Samuel, 'Looks aren't everything. Don't be impressed with his looks and stature. I've already eliminated him. God judges persons differently than humans do. Men and women look at the face; God looks into the heart'" (1 Sam. 16:7 MSG).
- "When you search for me, you will find me; if you seek me with all your heart" (Jer. 29:13).
- "I'm absolutely convinced that nothing—nothing living or dead, angelic or demonic, today or tomorrow, high or low, thinkable or unthinkable—absolutely *nothing* can get

between us and God's love because of the way that Jesus our Master has embraced us" (Rom. 8:39 MSG).

- "The world is unprincipled. It's dog-eat-dog out there! The world doesn't fight fair. But we don't live or fight our battles that way—never have and never will. The tools of our trade aren't for marketing or manipulation, but they are for demolishing that entire massively corrupt culture. We use our powerful God-tools for smashing warped philosophies, tearing down barriers erected against the truth of God, fitting every loose thought and emotion and impulse into the structure of life shaped by Christ. Our tools are ready at hand for clearing the ground of every obstruction and building lives of obedience into maturity" (2 Cor. 10:3–6 MSG).

- "Don't become so well-adjusted to your culture that you fit into it without even thinking. Instead, fix your attention on God. You'll be changed from the inside out. Readily recognize what he wants from you, and quickly respond to it. Unlike the culture around you, always dragging you down to its level of immaturity, God brings the best out of you, develops well-formed maturity in you" (Rom. 12:2 MSG).

CHAPTER 2

KNOW THE ENEMY

"Discipline yourselves, keep alert. Like a roaring lion your adversary the devil prowls around, looking for someone to devour"

(1 Pet. 5:8).

Have you seen the commercial where the announcer warns us that we are in danger of becoming "nose blind" to the smells around us? A hapless teenager does not recognize the putrid smell of his athletic socks, since he has become used to their odor.

The same numbing may happen to other senses as well. Repetition dulls reality. Take, for instance, my son. When he was in high school, it was impossible to find an alarm clock that woke that boy up. Any given alarm worked for a while but always became ineffective. Eventually he didn't even hit the snooze button anymore; he slept through the noise. He became so attuned to the alarm it no longer woke him from his sleep.

Similarly, we become "blind" to the lies that are repeatedly launched at us from the world. Perhaps having heard certain lies for so long we do not hear the alarm when the mistruth slips into our psyche. The enemy's voice becomes so familiar that it starts to sound like our own. The battle becomes so subtle that we do not realize we are at war. For me, the voice of incompetence has knocked around in my head so long that when I call myself an idiot, it sounds like the truth. I do not hear the alarm warning me it is a lie.

Our hope rests in becoming attuned to the voice of truth (God's Word) so we recognize the voice of the lie (Satan). This battleground of truth versus lie is not always apparent. The apostle Paul warned us that we are not struggling against flesh and blood but against rulers and power of the spiritual realms (Eph. 6:12). Paul's warning has always unnerved me out a bit, but isn't it good to know what we are up against?

Ha. I do not think we have a clue what we are up against.

Our battles are not against people, objects, or circumstances. The problem is not our neighbor, our boss, or the stock market. Satan may use such aspects of life, but they are only weapons. Oftentimes, we unwittingly cooperate with his efforts. Though we may not be our own worst enemy, we are capable of being an accomplice of our worst enemy.

To properly engage in the battle, we need to know more about the enemy. We need to recognize that Satan is real and that he is powerful. Our modern sensibilities may poo-poo the idea of an evil spiritual being who is out to get us. He is not akin to the boogieman, a wicked witch, or a haunted house. He and his minions are much subtler and scarier. He will knock on your front door and while you are answering it, he will come around to your back door and rob you blind. He does not fight fairly.

We get a glimpse of the reality and power of the warfare waged in the heavenly realms in the story of Daniel. Daniel received a troubling vision concerning a great war (Dan. 10:1), and went into a period of mourning, fasting, and praying. In response to Daniel's prayer, God sent a heavenly messenger; however, the messenger took three weeks to arrive. He told Daniel that he would have been there sooner, but he was delayed by Satan for those three weeks.

Paul too talks about being delayed by the devil. He tried to return to the church in Thessalonica but was repeatedly blocked: "For we wanted to come to you—certainly I, Paul, did, again and again—but Satan blocked our way" (1 Thess. 2:18).

Some may write off the idea of spiritual forces as the result of a healthy imagination or creative storytelling, but that thinking only plays into Satan's hands. He loves it when we underestimate him. Any military strategist will maintain that it is fatal to sell the enemy's strengths short. Satan wants us to believe we can win the battle on our own—with good behavior, good works, will power, and reason. Jesus's follower Peter says, "Be alert and of sober mind. Your enemy the devil prowls around like a roaring lion looking for someone to devour" (1 Pet. 5:8 NIV).

You would think a roaring lion would be easy to detect—but not if we have gone "alarm blind." Peter is not describing cuddly; he is describing cunning. To shrug off the enemy as a pushover when he is armed, organized, experienced, determined, and dangerous is to invite defeat.

He says we are worthless, and we agree. We beat ourselves up with guilt, assuming grace is for everyone else but us. He tricks us into believing the lie that there is no sense even engaging in the fight. We are not worth the trouble and effort. We will never win. He shifts our focus to see our sin, not our Savior.

Do not underestimate him. Do you realize the peril you are in?

Neither should we overestimate him. God invites us to remember who is fighting on our side. We are to "be strong in the Lord and in the strength of his power" (Eph. 6:10). In our corner is the God of angel armies, the almighty, zealous, fierce, and powerful Father who says yes, we are worth fighting for—and he did just that. The prophet Isaiah tells us that nothing formed against God can stand, and therefore nothing formed against us can stand unless God allows it (Isa. 54:17). Expect success. Take a stand against the devil's schemes with the armor of God clad around your souls. (See chapter 6 for more on the armor of God.)

One time during my prayers, I was face-down before God, heartbroken over a senseless tragedy where many innocent lives were lost, and it felt like pure evil to me. I sank into the depths of despair, and I asked God, "How can you stand this? You know of this evil and even more that I'm not even aware of. If this breaks my heart, how can it not devastate yours?" And I heard, clear as a bell, God say to me, "Because I know how all of this ends."

This truth has stuck with me. In the end, all will be well—and if all is not well, then it is not the end.[2] Yes, while we wait for God to bring about his kingdom on Earth, Satan is the prince of this world. In this age, he has power. The Bible says Satan is the ruler of the kingdom of Earth, the whole world is under his control, and, as the god of this age, he has blinded people (Eph. 2:1–2, 1 John 5:19; 2 Cor. 4:4).

His weapon is deception (John 8:44). Jesus describes Satan as the father of lies. Lying is his native tongue. He has the capability and the desire to influence people with the allure of possessions, power, and pleasure. His influence is personal and corporate. It encompasses governments, cultures, and commerce. Evil schemes and false religions are under his control, having sprung from his deceptions. The darkness is inward and outward. The goal is to destroy (John 10:10).

No wonder we are such a mess.

But before we despair, remember: God has the last word. God is still ultimately in control. According to his wisdom, God has put boundaries for Satan in place, and those who walk in the truth are safely within those boundaries. "He has rescued us from the power of darkness and transferred us into the kingdom of his beloved Son" (Col. 1:13). Satan is on a leash, so to speak.

For instance, Satan had to ask Jesus's permission to shake the faith of Jesus's friend Peter. Just before his death, Jesus tells Peter that the enemy "has demanded to sift all of you like wheat" (Luke 22:31). Satan wanted to shake the faith of Jesus's friends in hopes they would fall away, like chaff separated from a kernel of wheat on the threshing floor, but Satan could not even tempt them without Jesus's permission. With Peter's faith restored after a grievous betrayal of Christ, he was stronger than ever and became the rock upon which the church was built. A rock so solid that the "gates of Hades" cannot overcome it (Matt. 16:18).

Satan made a similar request of God regarding the prophet Job. Satan was not allowed to touch Job without God's permission. Satan drops in for a visit with God in heaven, and God points to Job's righteous lifestyle as proof one could live as God designed his creation to live—dependent upon and completely satisfied with God. Satan says it is only because God has blessed Job so much. Take it all away, Satan dares, and watch the cursing begin.

Satan was convinced Job was a "rice Christian," a term used to describe those who are not really interested in the message of the missionary, only in the missionary's food. God allowed Satan to take away all of Job's "rice" and then watched. Job did not curse God. Sure, there was suffering, questioning, and lamenting. Yet, "in all this Job did not sin or charge God with wrongdoing." Job said, "the Lord *gave, and the* Lord *has taken away; blessed be the name of the Lord"* (Job 1:21–22).

Satan loves the idea of rice Christians.

Some might argue that it is downright reckless and risky of God to allow the devil and evil princes to roam around and have power on the earth. Evidently God has a role for Satan or Satan would be gone, which he will be at the end of the age. Remember, Satan has no hold over us if we reject his lies and believe the truth, just as he had no hold over Jesus, who said, "the ruler of this world is coming. He has no power over me" (John 14:30).

We live in the paradox of the "meantime." God has won the war over death and darkness but has not yet returned to establish his everlasting kingdom on earth. God, in Jesus, came to earth and rewrote the end of our story, but we haven't reached the last page yet. God's preferred future has not yet been fully realized. So, in the meantime, our warfare in this world refines our faith like fire refines gold and we are brought closer to God because of it. I am not saying God causes hardships. Stuff happens. But if he wants to put us through a trial, he will. He's God after all. He can do what he wants.

Peter speaks of trials that come so "that our faith—of greater worth than gold—may result in praise, glory, and honor" (1 Pet. 1:7). Satan's purpose for opposing us is to consume us in the fire of trials, temptations, and accusations. God's purpose is for good. If we can avoid becoming bitter, we become better. Refined, pure, useful, and glowing—a light living for God's glory.

Whenever I have been in a group where we discuss the hardships of life, I ask whether we would, if given the chance, go back in time and change a particularly difficult period of our lives. To this point, participants have said no, because the hardship has made them who they are today and brought them closer to God.

Now we know a little more about the enemy, but where exactly is the battlefield? We think we will have time to gear up for the fight when we see it coming, but the time to put on the armor is now, because the battle is at hand. The battlefield is everywhere: at home, work, church, out with friends. It surfaces when stress is high and health is failing. It emerges in righteous anger and low self-esteem. It crops up in courtrooms and checkbooks, in front of mirrors, and under the table.

The question is not whether we want to be in this war. The battle is at hand. The question is this: Will we let Satan's lies pierce our armor in defeat, or will we share in the victorious life God has already secured for us?

For Personal or Group Study:

Thoughts to Consider

- In what ways have you become "alarm blind"?
- What comes to mind when you hear that your enemy is of the spiritual realm?
- In what ways have you been an accomplice to Satan?
- What hardships or trials have you endured? Did they drive you closer or farther away from God?
- Describe how hardships and trials have made you the person you are today.
- Are you a "rice Christian," believing that God has promised you an easy life if you follow him?

Detect the Lie

- Satan is not real or powerful.
- The idea of warfare in a spiritual realm is the result of an overactive imagination.
- If God really loved me, he would keep me from facing trials and temptations.
- The hardships of life show me that I need to have a tough exterior.
- I will engage in the battle when I am ready.

Argue against the Lie

- The battle is raging now.

- It is easy to go "alarm blind" to the lies of this world.

- Satan and his forces are real and cunning.

- God uses trials to refine us, not defeat us.

- God has given us armor for the battle.

- God is on our side. He is a contender for us.

- Our hope rests in becoming attuned to the voice of truth so that we become aware of and recognize the voice of the lie.

- Satan only has power in this world because God allows it.

Replace the Lie with the Truth (God's Word)

- "Discipline yourselves, keep alert. Like a roaring lion your adversary the devil prowls around, looking for someone to devour" (1 Pet. 5:8).

- "My dear children, you come from God and belong to God. You have already won a big victory over those false teachers, for the Spirit in you is far stronger than anything in the world" (1 John 4:4 MSG).

- "The Son of God was revealed for this purpose, to destroy the works of the devil" (1 John 3:8).

- "Now is the judgment of this world; now the ruler of this world will be driven out" (John 12:31).

- "So take everything the Master has set out for you, well-made weapons of the best materials. And put them to use so you will be able to stand up to everything the Devil throws your way. This is no afternoon athletic contest that we'll walk away from and forget about in a couple of hours. This is for keeps, a life-and-death fight to the finish against the Devil and all his angels" (Eph. 6:10–12 MSG).

- "We know that we are from God, and the whole world lies in the power of the evil one" (1 John 5:19 ESV).

- "It wasn't so long ago that you were mired in that old stagnant life of sin. You let the world, which doesn't know the first thing about living, tell you how to live. You filled your lungs with polluted unbelief, and then exhaled disobedience" (Eph. 2:1–2 MSG).

- "No weapon that is fashioned against you [God] shall prosper, and you shall confute every tongue that rises against you in judgment" (Isa. 54:17).

- "I will no longer talk much with you, for the ruler of this world is coming. He has no power over me; but I do as the Father has commanded me, so that the world may know that I love the Father" (John 14:30–31).

- "He has rescued us from the power of darkness and transferred us into the kingdom of his beloved Son, in whom we have redemption, the forgiveness of sins" (Col. 1:13–14).

- "And no wonder! Even Satan disguises himself as an angel of light. So it is not strange if his ministers also disguise themselves as ministers of righteousness. Their end will match their deeds" (2 Cor. 11:14–15).

CHAPTER 3

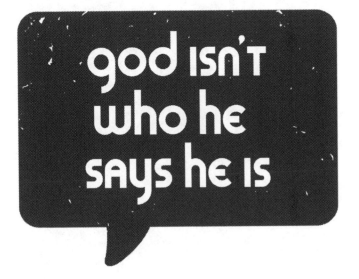

"God is not a human being, that he should lie, or a mortal, that he should change his mind. Has he promised, and will he not do it? Has he spoken, and will he not fulfill it?"

(Num. 23:19).

et's look at a fictional friend, Debra. She is in a funk. She feels guilty for her state of emotions. The adage "it could be worse" runs through her head, which only adds weight to the load she carries. "Why do I feel this way?" she laments.

Her inclination is to blame someone or something else. Her husband is not as attentive as he used to be. Who can blame him when she cannot lose weight, because she is a failure when it comes to dieting? She feels lonely when she tries to talk about her problems with her girlfriends. They do not understand.

Where is God? She prays, or at least tries to pray, but nothing ever changes. In fact, the problems worsen. Maybe she is getting what she deserves.

This situation may sound familiar. We all have circumstances in our lives we would like to change—the only difference is the list of problems and their causes. Yet some people seem to navigate life's problems with ease, like a canoe cutting through rapids. What is their secret? Is it because they have found favor with God? We may mistakenly believe God's abundance is a bowlful of trouble-free tokens we cash in when life's waters become choppy.

That is not the case. The abundant living Christ promises us is not free from troubles. Instead, abundant living in Christ is the ability to traverse the realities of life—like loneliness, rejection, and disappointments—with joy and grace.

How do we get that life?

The difference between a victorious life and a defeated life rests in recognizing the lies we believe about ourselves and about God. When those lies are identified, argued against, and replaced with the truth, that life is not only achievable, but—as Jesus promised—is ours. A life not defeated by low self-esteem and heightened turmoil, but a life that is satisfying, fulfilled, and abundant (John 10:10).

As we have learned, Satan, the father of lies, is the source of our misbeliefs. He has a double-edged sword of deception. One side of the blade wields the lie that God is not who he says he is; the other side of the blade wields the lie that we are not who God says we are.

To understand, let us begin at the beginning: Genesis, chapters 2–3. There once was a tree in a garden. God tells the occupants of the garden—Adam and Eve—that they are free to eat from any tree, just not the Tree of the Knowledge of Good and Evil. Eating the fruit of this tree will result in death.

Along comes Satan, and he gets the ear of Eve. "Did God really say you can't eat from any tree in the garden?" he asks.

"Oh no," she says, "any tree is fine. Just not that tree." She points to the one in the middle. "God said we may not eat of it or touch it. If we do, we'll die."

"Certainly, you won't die!" says the serpent. "God doesn't want you to know things, that's all. He doesn't want your eyes to be opened for fear you'll be as he is, knowing good and evil."

The fruit did look rather good. And who doesn't want wisdom? So Eve ate from the tree and gave Adam a bite. Both of their eyes were opened, and they realized they were naked.

Did you catch the lie in the story? Did you notice how it starts small—so small that we often miss it? Satan's first question to Eve is, "Did God say you should not eat of any tree in the garden?" The seed of doubt is planted. God did not say they could not eat of any tree, only one tree. Satan makes humankind doubt and explain God.

Satan also shifts their focus. Never mind the other trees that are freely available, completely adequate, and incredibly good. He tricks Eve and Adam into concentrating on the one that is off limits.

Satan employs this proven strategy today. Evangelist Oswald Chambers, in his devotional *My Utmost for His Highest,* says, "Satan . . . does not come to us on the premise of tempting us to sin, but on the premise of shifting our point of view."[3]

Satan knows any prospect of limitation bothers us. Sometimes we do not want something until we are told we cannot have it.

Put a pile of gold-wrapped candies and a pile of silver-wrapped candies in front of a group of children and tell them they can eat all the gold ones they want, but the silver ones are off limits. Which one will they gravitate toward? The silver ones must be special, and they want to know why. They become suspicious: "What are the adults hiding from us?"

Notice too the difference between what God says of the tree and what Eve says of the tree. God says they are not allowed to eat from it, but Eve adds an additional limitation, saying they cannot even touch it. Truth is pushed to the margins, and it does not take long for Satan to shove it off the page. He says, "You certainly will not die," if you eat of the fruit.

A lie is born, and death enters our story, for the wages of sin is death (Rom. 6:23). Satan's twisting of the truth leads Adam and Eve to believe that God does not want them to eat of the tree because he tries to keep them out of the loop. They become suspicious of God, and this lie that God cannot be trusted cascades down to all generations. We too may be suspicious of God and wonder, "What is God hiding from us?"

Satan convinces us that if God had our best interests in mind, he would not make anything off limits. "For God knows" (Gen. 3:5), he says—insinuating that God knows we will be happier, fulfilled, and powerful if we just take that bite of disobedience. Satan convinces us that God is afraid we will no longer need him if we know the truth. Satan convinces us that disobedience is better than servitude to a God who does not care or is not adequate.

Satan says to Eve, "Did God really say . . .?" And he continues to speak those words to our hearts today. Did God really say you were his masterpiece, fearfully and wonderfully made (Ps. 139:14)? Did God really say you are free and forgiven? Did God really say you are his child (Eph. 1:5)?

Satan warps our sense of who God is. By questioning God's character and intention, he invites us to believe falsehoods about God's identity and purpose.

Throughout my life, God has morphed into many different roles—and most of them serve my selfishness. Always, my god is too small. I attempt to make him in my image and bring him down to my level. I guess it is human nature to resist a God who makes too many demands upon me.

Growing up, I created a vending-machine God. With this version of God, all I had to do was obey the rules and pull the right levers. Author and speaker Donald Miller describes this in his book *Blue Like Jazz:*

> To me, God was more of an idea. It was something like a slot machine, a set of spinning images that doled out rewards based on behavior and, perhaps, chance. This

slot-machine God provided a relief for the pinging guilt and a sense of hope that my life would get organized toward a purpose. I was too dumb to test the merit of the slot machine idea. I simply began to pray for forgiveness, thinking the cherries might line up and the light atop the machine would flash, spilling shiny tokens of good fate. What I was doing was more in line with superstition than spirituality. But it worked. If something nice happened to me, I thought it was God, and if something nice didn't, I went back to the slot machine, knelt down in prayer, and pulled the lever a few more times. I liked this God very much because you hardly had to talk to it and it never talked back.[4]

For some people, God is more like a managing director. His job is to coordinate and steer the universe and make sure everything comes out okay in the end. He is not so much involved in the details of our lives. He is a big-picture guy, working everything out on a super-cosmic level.

Maybe God is a cosmic police officer, and his primary duty is to catch us when we are doing something wrong and scold us with a wagging finger that showers us with guilt.

Or perhaps God is a caretaker who exists to serve you, described best in cat and dog theology. A dog says, "You pet me, you feed me, you shelter me, you love me, you must be God." A cat says, "You pet me, you feed me, you shelter me, you love me, I must be God."[5]

If you know anything about cats and dogs, you know how true this contrast is. It is said that dogs have masters and cats have staff. In the "theology" department, both the dog and cat believe in God, but each has a quite different view of who he is. Cats want to know, "What's in it for me?" and seek God for what he can do for them, and not for who he is. Dogs just love God because he's God, and seek him for who he is, not for what he can do for them.

Many concepts of God exist that fall short or go awry of who God has revealed himself to be through Scripture and his Son, Jesus. Satan wields his double-edged sword of lies, attempting to sever us from the truth.

Remember our friend Debra? Satan has her right where he wants her—believing that God has left her to her own devices. He has her believing that God does not really care about her and that if she could only be "more," then maybe God will give her the life she deserves. He has her believing her happiness is dependent on people and circumstances. He whispers in her ear with a scoff: "Did God really say your worth was determined by him, and not by your husband, friends, weight, or circumstances?"

If we are planted firmly in the truth of who God is—and who we are to him—we can resoundingly respond, "Yes! God really did say my worth was determined by him."

For Personal or Group Study:

Thoughts to Consider

- Is it true that limitations bother you?
- What doubts do you have that finish the question, "Did God really say...?"
- Have you witnessed, in yourself or someone else, a "slow fade" where wrongdoing started small but grew to troublesome levels?

- How is misbelief different from unbelief?
- What do you think Jesus meant when he promised you an abundant life?
- How would you describe your view of God? Has it changed as you have grown? How has it changed?
- Where do you go to learn the truth about who God is?

Detect the Lie

- An abundant life is too much to ask for.
- My life's circumstances will improve if I can gain God's favor.
- God is not as loving as he would like us to believe.
- There are prerequisites to worthiness.
- God is not that interested in the details of my life. He has bigger concerns than me.

Argue against the Lie

- Satan tries to shift your focus from the true goodness and love of God.
- God's only motivation is love.
- God is who he says he is.
- Jesus and God's Word are two ways God's character is revealed to you.
- God is intimately involved in every detail of your life.
- You can trust God.
- He always has your best interests in mind.

Replace the Lie with the Truth (God's Word)

- "All you need to remember is that God will never let you down; he'll never let you be pushed past your limit; he'll always be there to help you come through it" (1 Cor. 10:13 MSG).

- "God means what he says. What he says goes. His powerful Word is sharp as a surgeon's scalpel, cutting through everything, whether doubt or defense, laying us open to listen and obey. Nothing and no one is impervious to God's Word. We can't get away from it—no matter what" (Heb. 4:12–13 MSG).

- "God is not a human being, that he should lie, or a mortal, that he should change his mind. Has he promised, and will he not do it? Has he spoken, and will he not fulfill it?" (Num. 23:19).

- "Beloved, let us love one another, because love is from God; everyone who loves is born of God and knows God" (1 John 4:7).

- "He [God] will rejoice over you with gladness, he will renew you in his love; he will exult over you with loud singing" (Zeph. 3:17).

- "Great is the Lord, and greatly to be praised; his greatness is unsearchable. One generation shall laud your works to another, and shall declare your mighty acts. On the glorious splendor of your majesty, and on your wondrous works, I will meditate. The might of your awesome deeds shall be proclaimed, and I will declare your greatness" (Ps. 145:3–6).

CHAPTER 4

WE ARE NOT who god says WE ARE

"But now thus says the Lord, he who created you, O Jacob, he who formed you, O Israel: Do not fear, for I have redeemed you; I have called you by name, you are mine. Because you are precious in my sight, and honored, and I love you"

(Isa. 43:1, 4).

Before I was called to ordained ministry, I was the editor-in-chief of a local parenting magazine. One of the first articles I wrote was about Reactive Attachment Disorder, which affects children who do not bond with a caregiver in their first years of life. They experience a world that does not meet their needs. They cry and are not comforted; they are hungry and are not immediately fed. Their experiences lead them to believe they cannot trust others to take care of them, so they must take matters into their own hands. Because they believe no one can be trusted, they find it extremely difficult to bond with other people. In other words, they have trust issues.

When it comes to our relationship with God, we too, have trust issues. We have looked at one side of Satan's double-edged sword, which is to get us to believe God is not who he says he is. The other side of the blade tries to sever us from the belief that we are who God says we are.

Jesus was baptized in the River Jordan, and no sooner had the water dripped off his brow than the Spirit of God comes upon him and God says, "This is my Son, the Beloved, with whom I am well pleased" (Matt. 3:17).

Immediately, Jesus's sandals hit the desert, where he fasts for forty days. Satan shows up and speaks to his hunger, "If you are the Son of God, command these stones to become loaves of bread." Jesus does not fall for it. Satan tries again, "If you are the Son of God, throw yourself down" (Matt. 4:1–11). Again, Jesus knows better.

In the garden with Adam and Eve, Satan attacked God's character, but here in the desert with Christ, Satan knows better than to attack God's character, so he attacks Christ's identity. "If you are the Son of God..."

Those same words echo in our hearts today. "If you are a son or daughter of God, then...," and we finish the sentence. "Why do you suffer so? Why do you have doubts? Why aren't you more content? Why doesn't God answer your prayers?"

Just as Satan can distract us with what we cannot have, as he did in the garden with the tree, he can also distract us from our true identity by getting us to focus on our weaknesses, failures, and unmet needs. He invites us to judge ourselves on what we have done or not done, on what we have or do not have, on how we measure up to others. He shifts our focus. He takes advantage of our trust issues with God.

He leads us to believe we are not who God says we are.

When Jesus was baptized, he had not yet preached a message or uttered a parable. He had not made one glass of wine, healed a leper, or cast out a demon. Yet God says he is pleased with him and loves him. From the beginning, God's approval of Jesus was for who Jesus was, not for what he did. We too have that same promise. We are loved for who we are, not for what we have or have not done.

That is not necessarily our experience with life. From an early age, we learn that effort equals reward. If I clean my plate, I get dessert. If I do well in school, I get a good grade. Heck, if I just participate in a track meet and come in dead last, I earn a participation ribbon. If any sincere effort is not met with some kind of reward, we yell, "Unfair!"

No wonder it is hard for us to swallow this concept of being loved for no other reason than we exist.

When you have children, no matter what they do, they are yours (sometimes this fact is good news, sometimes not so much). Your children have your DNA. They are—and always will be—yours, regardless of what they say or do.

Baptism is a reminder that you have God's DNA in you. A baby has never put money in the offering plate, volunteered at a food pantry, or even burped "thank you" to a parent. Our children have done nothing to earn our love, much less the love of God. Yet they have our love, imperfect as it is, just as we have God's love, perfect as it is.

In 2013, three women who had been missing for more than a decade were found after a dramatic rescue just a few miles from where they were abducted. It ended years of anguished searching by the families and authorities. Amanda Berry, who was kidnapped at the age of sixteen, reached her arm through a crack in a front door and captured the attention of a passerby who heard her screams for help. Her rescuer kicked out the bottom of the door and Amanda crawled through. Eventually the other two were rescued and their kidnapper captured.

I do not think any of us can imagine what it was like for Amanda and her friends to have been taken away from their loved ones and forced to live against their will in another person's house. The longing to be reunited with their families must have been unbelievably intense. During this time, do you think any of the girls thought, "I need to get home so I can do my chores and clean my room. Imagine how far behind I am on my homework"? No. They were hungry for home because it is where they were loved. It is where they belonged.

What must have been going through the minds of their parents? During the ten years the girls were missing, did they think, "I wish our daughter was here to get her chores done, and clean her room, and get good grades so she could make us proud"? Absolutely not. They ached to have their daughters back because they were theirs. They loved their children and wanted them back where they belonged.

This sentiment, too, is the heart of God. He wants you to be home with him, where you belong—not because of what you can do for him, but because he loves you, because you are his child. If you cannot earn God's love, then you can do nothing to lose it. God's verdict on your life is this fact: "This is my child, in whom I am well pleased." Nothing you do can make God love you more; nothing you do can make God love you less. Pause for a moment and let that wash over you.

Satan is really good—an expert, actually—at getting us to believe our self-worth is rooted in our efforts, looks, IQ, social status, and more. He tells us we are naked and we must clothe ourselves with the standards the world has set, instead of don the garment of unconditional acceptance our Creator longs to wrap around our shoulders. "Remember," Satan whispers, "he can't be trusted. You had better take matters into your own hands."

We may mistakenly believe that our problems with God all stem from misbehavior or unruly thoughts. But the true root of our problems begins with believing the lies that God is not who he says he is and that we are not who God says we are.

One of my spiritual mentors is author and speaker Dr. Timothy Keller. He expounded on how our lack of trust in God leads to idolatry in an article "Talking about Idolatry in a Postmodern Age."[6] He uses Protestant reformer Martin Luther's Treatise on Good Works to make the case that if we break any commandment, it is because we first broke the most important one: "Love the

Lord your God with all your heart, soul, mind and strength" (Matt. 22:36–37).

Why do we lie? Usually to save face or advance our cause. When we lie, whatever we lied about becomes more important to us than God at that moment. Lying becomes our idol and is our attempt to take control of how others see us, to control our circumstances—or to control other people.

Why do we covet? Because we do not believe God has given us all we need. Whatever we covet has become our idol and is more important to us than God at that moment.

Early in my career, I often procrastinated. The joke in the office of the magazine I worked at was that I was going to write an article on procrastination but could never get it done. I thought the perfectly sane solution would be to have some blank pages saying, "Article on procrastination to come." I was alone in that opinion. My procrastination often caused me trouble. Someone would ask if I had completed a writing assignment, and rather than tell the truth I lied and said, "Yes." Why? Because I did not want anyone to think badly of me. I did not want to be perceived as inadequate, unorganized, or apathetic. My reputation became my idol and how others perceived me was more important to me than God at that moment. I had bought into the lie that my worth was based on another person's opinion of me. Now I can proudly say I am a graduate of Procrastinators Anonymous. (No, that group does not really exist. Who would schedule the meetings?)

If our identity is rooted in God's truth, we do not have to lie to cover up, covet because we compare, or put others down to feel lifted up. We would not murder with our thoughts, steal to gain possessions, or lust after others. We would be content with who we are, how we look, and what we have—basing our value in God's economy, not the world's.

Here is an example of how the world's economy works. If you are last in line at a concert, you are likely to find yourself in a back-row seat. If you are behind the crowd at a clearance sale, you will get merchandise that is picked over and not in your size. If you are a latecomer to an Easter buffet, the hotdish will be cold and the good desserts scarce.

It is a dog-eat-dog world out there, and you had better be willing to fight for the good things of life or get left behind. No one else is going to look out for you. That is the world's economy.

God's economy is different. Those who are last still find front-row seats. You do not have to fight for that sweater in your size because there are boxes of sweaters in the back room. The buffet table is overflowing with piping-hot hotdishes and an abundance of amazing desserts.

God never hands out consolation prizes and there is an endless supply of what we really need—love, time, and attention. You never have to prove you are deserving of any of them.

We do not necessarily like that because we want God to punish the bad guys, reward the good guys, and declare someone the winner. But that is not how he works.

Unfortunately, we are more aware of what we lack than we are of God's provisions. The problem underneath all our problems is we believe the lie of Satan over the truth of God.

Perhaps you are thinking, "OK, I get it. I resolve to love and trust God more." But here is the rub. That resolution puts the onus on you and your efforts, not on God and his love. So, what is a person to do?

Relax. God's love is yours, unearned and unconditional, even when your idols raise their ugly heads. Obey God's laws not because you want to look good, earn favor, or fear rejection, but because you have experienced the profound grace of a God who completes you—a God who is who he says he is and who loves you, warts and all. Let God transform your heart and mind until you believe that you can indeed trust God—he is who he says he is, and you are his beloved.

For Personal or Group Study:

Thoughts to Consider

- How easy is it for you to trust someone? Do they have to earn your trust first?
- What doubts do you have that finish the question, "If you are a child of God, then why . . .?" Do these doubts still echo in your heart today?
- How does Satan distract you from what you have/do not have?
- How does Satan distract you from who you are/are not?
- What weakness does Satan take advantage of in your life?
- Can you think of an example when your sin was a result of breaking the first commandment?

Detect the Lie

- I cannot trust God.
- I am loved for what I do, not for who I am.
- I can lose God's love if I am not careful.

- I need to look out for myself. No one else will do it for me.
- God loves everyone else but I'm not sure he loves me.
- I am a disappointment to God.

Argue against the Lie

- I am who God says I am—his beloved.
- God has gone to great lengths to show me I am his.
- God's DNA is in me and no matter what I do, I am his child.
- I cannot lose his love.
- God desires to bring me to himself, home—where I belong.

Replace the Lie with the Truth (God's Word)

- "So let God work his will in you. Yell a loud *no to the Devil and watch him scamper. Say a quiet yes to God and he'll be there in no time*" (James 4:7 MSG).

- "Teacher, which commandment in the law is the greatest?" He said to him, "'You shall love the Lord your God with all your heart, and with all your soul, and with all your mind'" (Matt. 22:36–37).

- "Desperate, I throw myself on you: *you* are my God! Hour by hour I place my days in your hand, safe from the hands out to get me. Warm me, your servant, with a smile; save me because you love me" (Ps. 31:14–16 MSG).

- "God's loyal love couldn't have run out, his merciful love couldn't have dried up. They're created new every morning. How great your faithfulness! I'm sticking

with God (I say it over and over). He's all I've got left"
(Lam. 3:22–24 MSG).

- "Oh, taste and see that the Lord is good; blessed is the one
  who trusts in him" (Ps. 34:8 NIV).

- "For I am the Lord your God, who takes hold of your
  right hand and says to you, 'Do not fear; I will help you'"
  (Isa. 41:13 NIV).

CHAPTER 5

"They exchanged the truth about God for a lie, and worshiped and served created things rather than the Creator—who is forever praised. Amen"

(Rom. 1:25 NIV).

In first grade, we were given a Styrofoam cup full of dirt. We parted the dirt with our little fingers and gingerly placed a bean seed about an inch down into the container. Then we brushed the soil over the seed, gave it a little water, and were encouraged to take the cup home, nurture it, and report what happened.

I was proud of my mini-garden and checked it many times a day, waiting to celebrate the bean's emergence. Finally, one day, green sprouts peaked through the dirt. I was so excited. I continued watering and coaxing growth until one day my dad walked by and said, "You realize you're growing a bunch of weeds, don't you?"

How could this be true? I took my cup back to my teacher, and sure enough, she confirmed my dad's verdict. I am not sure why my bean seed failed to thrive when useless seeds that produced useless weeds did. I was sad.

There I sat, with my cup of weeds. No matter how much I wished the weeds were a beanstalk, they never would be. The only way for weeds to become beans is to change the roots.

In his book *The 7 Habits of Highly Effective People*, American educator Stephen Covey says, "In the words of Thoreau, 'For every thousand hacking at the leaves of evil, there is one striking at the root.' We can only achieve the quantum improvements in our lives as we quit hacking at the leaves of attitude and behavior and get to work on the root, the paradigm, from which our attitudes and behaviors flow."[7]

It is useless to repeatedly try to change how we act and think without looking at the deeper reasons for our thoughts and actions. If we fail to "strike at the root"—the lies we have allowed to grow in our soul—we will end up with a pile of worthless weeds.

Let us look at another fictional friend, Sebastian. He was a successful businessman with a loving wife and family, a fine athlete, and a lover of a great steak cooked on the grill. Yet, he was having problems with his self-esteem, so he sought counseling. After a few sessions, it became clear that his low self-esteem stemmed from his overbearing and overcritical parents. He was never good enough to get their approval. They often shamed him for his decisions and actions. After many years of struggling, he came to believe what his parents said about him—he could never measure up and he should be ashamed of himself.

However, Sebastian's parents had been dead for years. How could they still be the problem? Their criticism of him was silenced years ago when they passed away.

The root of his problems was not his parents, but the fact he had bought into the lies his parents told him about himself. He was in bondage to circumstances that were long over. He had allowed mistruths of his past to shape his present self-image, and therefore his present emotional health.

After this realization, and through some hard work of the soul, Sebastian was able to free himself from self-loathing and live an emotionally stable and fulfilling life.

Sebastian was able to free himself from a stronghold of shame—not by forgetting what his parents said, but by changing what he told himself about what they said. He had believed a lie. When he recognized and argued against the lie, he was able to replace it with the truth and was freed.

What we tell ourselves about who we are can be one of two options: 1) the truth, or 2) a lie. Christian counselors William

Backus and Marie Chapian, in their book *Telling Yourself the Truth,* developed a misbelief therapy that uncovered the root of the truth/ lie distinction.[8] I call this process "The Lie Detector." You've already been introduced to it in previous chapters, but let's expound on its usage:

1. Detect the lie.

    a. What is causing your negative emotions?

    b. What assumptions are you making about yourself, others and/or God?

    c. What destructive words, thoughts, or actions support the lie?

2. Argue against the lie.

    a. Ask, "Who told you that . . .?" about yourself, others, and/or God.

    b. Does it accurately reflect God's character? ("Did God really say . . .?")

    c. Does it accurately define your identity? ("If you are a child of God . . .?")

3. Replace the lie with the truth.

    a. The truth is consistent with Scripture (John 17:17).

    b. The truth will bring peace, light, constructive thoughts, and love (1 Cor. 13:6; 1 Pet. 1:22).

    c. The truth will set you free (John 8:32).

How would this process have played out for Sebastian?

- Detect the lie: he believed what his parents said about him was true.

- Argue against the lie: he argued that their opinion of him was not based in truth but on their unrealistic expectations of him and perhaps their own pain.

- Replace the lie with the truth: he acknowledged that God decides his worth, not other people—not even his parents.

The beauty of The Lie Detector is that you can see immediate results. You can have the abundant life Jesus promises now. You can be freed of a false self-image today. You can quiet self-destructive thoughts and attitudes immediately. Self-examination and honesty mixed with the truth, which is the Word of God, has the potential to change your life.

This method has helped me tremendously. I have allowed lies and misbeliefs to victimize me my whole life. The following is an example of how I used The Lie Detector after an event sent me down the path of self-doubt. I was leading a meeting that was going awry. No one had done what I had asked, and I was frustrated because deadlines were looming. I came down on the crew gathered around the table pretty hard. After my rant, the room was dead silent. They all looked down at their notebooks and did not say a word. "Great!" I thought. "They all are hating me right now. I really blew it." I adjourned the meeting and walked out of the room.

I left the meeting angry, and my mood did not improve as the day went on. My frustration shifted from being annoyed at others to being annoyed at myself, because I handled the situation poorly. I started thinking to myself, "Well, this just proves you are not good at motivating others," and, "I'm pretty sure they all think I'm a bitch." By evening, I was in a foul mood.

Fortunately, I remembered The Lie Detector, so I stopped my spinning mind and used it. I said to myself:

1. What is the lie?

    a. I am a terrible leader.

    b. Everyone is judging me, and they find me lacking.

    c. Because I acted stupidly, they don't like me now and never will again.

2. Then, I argued against the lie.

    a. Yes, perhaps I could have handled the meeting better, but I believe God has called and equipped me to be in the leadership position I am in.

    b. I know everyone in that room loves me and I love them. One meeting will not change that.

3. And, I replaced the lie with the truth.

    a. One meeting does not define me or my abilities.

    b. The people in that room do not define me or determine my worth.

    c. God defines me, accepts me, and loves me.

    d. I may have made a mistake, but that comes with being human.

    e. I can always ask for forgiveness and try again tomorrow. Done.

Stopping for a few minutes to challenge the lies made a huge difference in my ability to sleep that night.

The Lie Detector is more than encouraging affirmations. It strikes at the root of the weeds in our life—the lies—and replaces them with the truth of who and whose we are.

Changing the root is a process, not an event, but we do not have to take on this challenge alone. We have the Spirit of truth as our guide and help and he wants to give us the fruit of the Spirit—love, joy, peace, patience, kindness, generosity, faithfulness, gentleness, and self-control (Gal. 5:22–23). But we must be a willing participant, by admitting change is possible. Rid yourself of "I can't change the way I am!" As long as you have convinced yourself you cannot change, you won't even try. Approach your self-talk and self-image with openness and honesty.

Barbara Cawthorne Crafton, an Episcopal priest, spiritual director, and author, says,

> All our exiles are self-imposed. It's not our guilty lists of thou-shalt-nots that cast us out: we cast ourselves out. We can't go home if we won't admit we're lost. We can't get better if we won't admit we're sick—we can't even try. "There's nothing wrong with me," we say angrily, "it's him, it's her, it's them, it's someone else. It's not me. I didn't do it. How dare you even suggest such a thing?" We think that admitting to our shortcomings dooms us. No. What dooms us is refusing to admit to them. And none of this is punishment from God—the estrangement of sin comes solely from us. Every last sorry bit of it.[9]

Over and over, Jesus tells people to believe, have faith, and trust. He said, "According to your faith let it be done to you" (Matt. 9:29). Faith is the act of believing. Jesus teaches us that what you believe has a direct result on how you live. If you believe you are nothing but a failure and life is hopeless, you will live that way. Contrarily, if you believe that in spite of your mistakes and shortfalls, you are not a failure, you will live *that* way. According to your faith let it be done to you.

Your worth is based solely on the declaration of God: "For God so loved the world" (John 3:16). The world is people. You are "people." God loves people, God loves you, and nothing—no thing—can change that (Rom. 8:38–39).

He cannot wait for that truth to be at the center of your life, so let's strap on the belt of truth, take up our shield of faith, and fiercely battle against Satan's weapons of deceit.

For Personal or Group Study:

Thoughts to Consider

- What lies have you been nurturing and allowing to grow?
- How have those lies choked out the truth?
- What negative (and positive) emotions from your past have shaped your self-image?
- How do they still affect you today?
- Do you believe you really can change, or are you more inclined to believe, "I can't change the way I am"?
- Do you see how The Lie Detector may be helpful?
- Barbara Cawthorne Crafton says, "All our exiles are self-imposed." Explain what that means to you.

Detect the Lie

- I am unable to free myself from my past. My past defines me.
- I have no control over how I react to what happens to me.
- "Sticks and stones may break my bones, but words will never hurt me."
- No one will respect me—and I will not respect myself—if I admit my shortcomings.
- My past sins and failures will crush me.

Argue against the Lie

- Satan is the source of my misbeliefs.
- I can change my life by refusing to believe self-destroying lies.
- All have fallen short of perfection, and God's love and forgiveness are for all.
- "Death and life are in the power of the tongue" (Prov. 18:21).
- The Holy Spirit (the Spirit of truth) is your guide and helper.

Replace the Lie with the Truth (God's Word)

- "They bend their tongues like bows; they have grown strong in the land for falsehood, and not for truth; for they proceed from evil to evil, and they do not know me, says the LORD" (Jer. 9:3).

- "They exchanged the truth about God for a lie, and worshiped and served created things rather than the Creator—who is forever praised. Amen" (Rom. 1:25 NIV).

- "For as he thinks in his heart, so is he" (Prov. 23:7 NKJV).

- "Pleasant words are like a honeycomb, sweetness to the soul and health to the body" (Prov. 16:24).

- "How? you ask. In Christ. God put the wrong on him who never did anything wrong, so we could be put right with God" (2 Cor. 5:21 MSG).

- "Do not lie to one another, seeing that you have stripped off the old self with its practices and have clothed yourselves with the new self, which is being renewed in knowledge according to the image of its creator" (Col. 3:9–10).

- "I write to you, not because you do not know the truth, but because you know it, and you know that no lie comes from the truth" (1 John 2:21).

- "In the hope of eternal life that God, who never lies, promised before the ages began" (Titus 1:2).

- "If you love me, show it by doing what I've told you. I will talk to the Father, and he'll provide you another Friend so that you will always have someone with you. This Friend is the Spirit of Truth" (John 14:16 MSG).

- By contrast, the fruit of the Spirit is love, joy, peace, patience, kindness, generosity, faithfulness, gentleness, and self-control. There is no law against such things" (Gal. 5:22–23).

- Do not be conformed to this world, but be transformed by the renewing of your minds, so that you may discern what is the will of God—what is good and acceptable and perfect" (Rom. 12:2).

CHAPTER 6

The armor of god

"We use our powerful God-tools for smashing warped philosophies, tearing down barriers erected against the truth of God, fitting every loose thought and emotion and impulse into the structure of life shaped by Christ"

(2 Cor. 10:3–6 MSG).

When my youngest son started hockey, I had no idea what a *breezer* was. I learned quickly and came to appreciate all the padding my hockey player needed. I made sure he had every last bit of padding on before he went onto the ice. After all, it protected precious cargo—my child.

God too knew that we, his precious cargo, would need protecting, so he did not leave us defenseless. Satan may have his weapons of deceit (which we will examine closer in chapters 7–19), but we have God on our side—and he has already won. Our advantage is found in wielding the truth, which The Lie Detector uncovers. And on top of the truth, God provides us with layers of spiritual armor. As the apostle Paul writes,

> Therefore put on the full armor of God, so that when the day of evil comes, you may be able to stand your ground, and after you have done everything, to stand. Stand firm then, with the belt of truth buckled around your waist, with the breastplate of righteousness in place, and with your feet fitted with the readiness that comes from the gospel of peace. In addition to all this, take up the shield of faith, with which you can extinguish all the flaming arrows of the evil one. Take the helmet of salvation and the sword of the Spirit, which is the word of God. And pray in the Spirit on all occasions with all kinds of prayers and requests. With this in mind, be alert and always keep on praying for all the Lord's people (Eph. 6:10–18 NIV).

Let's look more closely at each piece of armor.

The belt of truth: For Roman soldiers, part of the battle gear was long flowing robes. Obviously, they did not think that fashion choice through. Any woman who has worn a long dress knows that long, flowing fabric around one's feet does one thing—trips you. For the soldiers to be able to fight without being tripped, they had to pick up their robes and tuck them into their belts. They had to "gird their loins."

Your loins are, obviously, an intimate part of your body, so we could read this passage to mean we are to take the truth and make it an intimate part of ourselves.

The whole of your armor rests upon this foundation—the truth. Girding our loins is to gather up our thoughts and live according to the truth, not according to the whims of our feelings or the lies of the enemy. We are invited to anchor our innermost parts to the truth. Take your scattered, confused, worried robe and stop tripping over it.

The breastplate of righteousness: While the belt is near your private organs, the breastplate covers your vital ones. From neck to waist, front to back, it protects the heart—the seat of your emotions and the center of your being.

The word "righteousness," simply put, means to be in a right relationship with God—being "right" with our Creator. It also means to be examined and to be found worthy. Who doesn't want that? Yet, deep down, we fear that if someone saw the "real me," they would at best be indifferent; at worst, be disgusted. And that might be especially true of God, who knows our inmost heart and intentions.

God is a holy God, and we are not, so of course he will find us unworthy. But when God looks at us, he sees his Son—because on the cross, Christ took our dirty robe of rebellion and exchanged it with his pure robe of righteousness. If we trust in the cross, we are right with God because Christ is right with God. It has nothing to do with how moral we are.

Paul was a moral, rule-following fellow before he met Jesus on the road to Damascus. He was a stellar Jew, doing all the right things. He goes through a list of all the reasons he could have crafted his own breastplate of righteousness, but he knew it would never be enough. He says, "I consider [all my credentials] garbage, that I may gain Christ and be found in him, not having a righteousness of my own that comes from the law, but that which is through faith in Christ—the righteousness that comes from God on the basis of faith" (Phil. 3:8–9 NIV).

We are not the ones who live a righteous life and offer it to God. Jesus is the One who lived a righteous life and offers it to us. Our righteousness, earned for us by Christ, causes the accusations of Satan to ping harmlessly against our breastplate and to fall to the floor.

The sandals of peace: When I played basketball in high school, my shoes were my most important equipment. If they were ill-fitting or if the traction was worn, I slipped around and lost footing at every turn. Shoes give you traction, protection, and mobility. Going into battle with slippery shoes would be fatal.

The sandals of peace represent our surefootedness—our confidence—the peace that comes from God. This peace helps us stand firm and protects us from the rocky and rough terrains of life.

The shield of faith: Have you ever watched a movie where a battle is raging and one side tries to climb their enemy's fortress, only to be met with hot tar being poured down on them? One fact is for sure—those climbing the walls are vulnerable, and a shield certainly would come in handy.

Roman soldiers carried shields that nearly covered their entire bodies. They used them in times of crisis, to shield off arrows, hot tar, and blows to the body. The shield of faith is to be used in times of crisis. It is our protection when arrows of doubt are flying our direction, when our self-esteem is taking hits, and when we are attempting to break down barriers in our life.

The helmet of salvation: We have talked about loins and hearts. Let us not forget the brain. Do not let Satan bring up your failures, flaws, or feelings of regret. I do not know who said this, but I like this adage: "When Satan starts to remind you of your past, remind him of his future."

Turn your thoughts to what awaits you. We are like a dirty cup being scrubbed cleaner and cleaner (sanctification), but no matter how hard we scrub, there will always be some coffee stains. That is the reality of life this side of heaven. But in our future salvation, which has already been secured for us by Jesus, even the coffee stains are gone. We will no longer live in the presence of sin but bask in the glory of God. Personally, I cannot wait. The helmet of salvation reminds us to have hope and to keep our mind on the prize—eternal life in the presence of God. Nothing here can compare to there. Nothing now can compare to then (Rom. 8:18).

The sword of the Spirit: We are told that the sword of the Spirit is the Word of God. A sword can be used defensively or offensively. The Word of God can inflict pain on the enemy and ward off the enemy's attacks. When Jesus was tempted in the wilderness, he warded off Satan's attacks with the Word of God.

Paul said this to his disciple Timothy: "There's nothing like the written Word of God for showing you the way to salvation through faith in Christ Jesus. Every part of Scripture is God-breathed and useful one way or another—showing us truth, exposing our rebellion, correcting our mistakes, training us to live God's way. Through the Word we are put together and shaped up for the tasks God has for us" (2 Tim. 3:16–17 msg).

Prayer: Paul concludes his armor speech by reminding us to pray—not because it is an afterthought, but because it holds all the armor together. Prayer is essential in the use of each weapon.

Truth, righteousness, peace, faith, salvation, God's Word, prayer: each a part of the arsenal that is ours. All we need to do is put the armor on. The battle is raging. Do not go into the fray unaware or unprepared.

Why would my son not put on his breezers, pads, and helmet—all that has been provided to protect him—before he entered the engagement on the ice? It would be foolish.

The armored one leads a victorious life. Paul reminds us:

The world is unprincipled. It's dog-eat-dog out there! The world does not fight fair. But we do not live or fight our battles that way—never have and never will. The tools of our trade are not for marketing or manipulation, but they are for demolishing that entire massively corrupt culture. We use our powerful God-tools for smashing warped philosophies, tearing down barriers erected against the truth of God, fitting every loose thought and emotion and impulse into the structure of life shaped by Christ. Our tools are ready at hand for clearing the ground of every obstruction

and building lives of obedience into maturity
(2 Cor. 10:3–6 MSG).

In warfare, tactics are the art and science of fighting battles.
Satan has many tactics, and he does not fight fairly. In the
following chapters, we will look at some of the ways the lies are
perpetuated—I call them weapons of deceit—and how to fight
against them. So, onward Christian soldiers! Let's gear up.

For Personal or Group Study:

Thoughts to Consider

- What feelings or past failures trip you up?
- Are you like Paul, crafting your own breastplate of righteousness?
- Can you name a time your faith shielded you?
- How does the knowledge of future salvation bring you hope and put life in perspective?
- What failures of your past does Satan bring up to steal your peace?
- Is prayer your first line of defense or your last line of defense?

Detect the Lie

- Life is a battle and God has left me defenseless.
- I can do battle using common sense, logic, and willpower.
- Prayer is a last resort. It is to be used when all else has failed.

- Reading the Word of God is not necessary; it is not relevant for today.
- The idea that a battle is raging is outdated and untrue.
- Knowing Scripture is not crucial to a victorious life.

Argue against the Lie

- The time to put on the armor is now.
- The foundation of the armor of God is the truth of who you are in Christ.
- Believing and knowing the Word of God is essential in our battle.
- You will live a defeated life without the armor of God.
- It is spiritually deadly to have a simplistic understanding of Satan.
- Jesus took the blows of Satan so I could have the righteousness of Jesus.

Replace the Lie with the Truth (God's Word)

- "His divine power has given us everything we need for a godly life through our knowledge of him who called us by his own glory and goodness" (2 Pet. 1:3).
- "For the word of God is alive and active. Sharper than any double-edged sword, it penetrates even to dividing soul and spirit, joints and marrow; it judges the thoughts and attitudes of the heart" (Heb. 4:12 NIV).

- "How? you ask. In Christ. God put the wrong on him who never did anything wrong, so we could be put right with God" (2 Cor. 5:21 MSG).

- "Therefore, since we have been justified through faith, we have peace with God through our Lord Jesus Christ" (Rom. 5:1).

- "For the weapons of our warfare are not of the flesh but have divine power to destroy strongholds" (2 Cor. 10:4 ESV).

- "For if, while we were God's enemies, we were reconciled to him through the death of his Son, how much more, having been reconciled, shall we be saved through his life!" (Rom. 5:10 NIV).

- "As God's chosen ones, holy and beloved, clothe yourselves with compassion, kindness, humility, meekness, and patience" (Col. 3:12).

- "Rejoice in hope, be patient in tribulation, be constant in prayer" (Rom. 12:12 ESV).

PART 2

⚡

Weapons
of Deceit

CHAPTER 7

"There is therefore now no condemnation for those who are in Christ Jesus"

(Rom. 8:1).

ears ago, we had a cat named Ozzie who did his best to keep the rabbit population in our yard under control. He knew where the baby bunnies nested and stalked them relentlessly. One day, he sauntered through a hole in our backdoor screen with a baby bunny in his mouth. (Please don't judge me.) Of course, when I saw Ozzie and the bunny I screamed. My scream startled the cat, who then dropped the bunny. The bunny took off and I screamed louder.

My brave husband rose to the occasion and tried to corner the baby bunny in the living room, but those little suckers are fast. I grabbed a flashlight, and we began to look under the furniture for our new "friend." But it was nowhere to be found. We thoroughly searched each room and as we determined a room to be bunny-free, we closed the door, trying to narrow down the places where the little critter could be hiding.

After a long search, we came up empty-handed. My husband did what every modern man does when faced with a dilemma: he Googled a solution. He learned that bunnies like strawberries and that one can use this fruit to lure them out of hiding. So that is what we did. We left one strawberry inside a live-capture trap in the basement. It seemed logical that the bunny had run downstairs. In addition, we left a strawberry on a plate in our son's room and shut the door. He was off to college, so we thought an extra trap couldn't hurt.

A week passed and we kept checking the basement trap. No bunny. (We did discover mice, but that is a whole 'nother story.) When our son came home for spring break, he walked out of his room, forehead furrowed with confusion, holding a plate and a limp bunny.

"Why is there a strawberry on a plate and a dead bunny in my room?"

Why am I telling you this story? Good question. Yes, I freaked out that there was a baby bunny running loose somewhere in my house, but the real trauma came when I shined a flashlight under couches and end tables. So much dust! The farther away from the epicenter of our living space, the thicker the "dust bunnies" (pun intended). I pride myself on keeping a clean house and was ashamed of the amount of dirt in the nooks and crannies of my home.

It made me think: What else am I ashamed of that I have hidden away in the nooks and crannies of my life? We all have past events we would not want anyone to shine a flashlight on. Incidents we would rather keep hidden, out of sight. Choices made that we regret. Secrets and shame that, if exposed, may devour us.

It is important to recognize shame as a weapon of deceit the devil uses to sabotage our relationship with God. Shame tells us we are bad and undeserving of freedom. While guilt's focus is on wrongdoing, shame's focus is on wrong-being. If guilt is not dealt with appropriately, it can turn into shame, and we become blinded to the truth of God's pardon. The root of the word "shame" derives from an older word meaning "to cover." In other words, we do not live up, so we cover up. If you hear a voice in your head that says, "You should be ashamed of yourself," ask yourself the question, "Who told me that?"

In 2004, Frank Warren, creator of The PostSecret Project, became fascinated with secrets. He printed around three thousand self-addressed postcards inviting people to share a secret with him—something that was true but that they had never told anyone. He handed these postcards out to people on the streets and encouraged people to mail them in. Slowly, secrets began showing up in his mailbox.

After several weeks he stopped handing out the postcards, but the secrets kept coming, some on postcards made from old photos, wedding invitations, or other personal items.

In 2012, he had a mountain of postcards in his basement divided into "bricks" of 250 postcards each. He estimated he has received more than half a million postcards—each with a secret that people had been too ashamed to share without anonymity.

Warren started a blog, "Postsecret.com." He scans a select few of the thousands he continues to receive each week and posts them.

Some are poignant. One written on the back of an envelope reads: "This envelope goes to the last Father's Day card I ever bought you, but I never got around to mailing it. You died 21 days later. I'll keep the card forever." A postcard with eight stamps says: "I found these stamps as a child, and I have been waiting all my life to have someone to send them to. I never did have someone." Another sender has a wish: "I wish I could throw all my 'friends' back into the lid of the box and choose all over again." This was written over a picture of a Scrabble game.

Some are humorous, like the Starbucks Styrofoam cup with these words written in black marker: "I give decaf to customers who are RUDE to me!" Or the postcard with a "No Outlet" street sign on the front, which reads, "My dad told me that this sign meant there were no outlet malls at the end of the street. I believed him until I was 12."

Others are quite somber, such as the secret written over a picture of someone snorting drugs: "I'm ashamed of how well

I've kept the fact that I'm a drug addict from my best friend." Or the crude drawing of an anorexic woman with the message: "I am happier when I am hungry." And the one that really blew my mind was a postcard with a hand-drawn picture of the Twin Towers in New York City burning on 9/11. It reads, "Everyone who knew me before 9/11 believes I'm dead."

Why do you suppose this invitation to send in secrets struck such a nerve with people? Warren says this: "We all have secrets: fears, regrets, hopes, beliefs, fantasies, betrayals, humiliations. We may not always recognize them but they are a part of us—like the dreams we can't always recall in the morning light." Warren comes to realize this truth: "After seeing thousands of secrets, I understand that sometimes when we believe we are keeping a secret, that secret is actually keeping us."[10]

Every day we decide what to reveal and what to conceal. While revelations can be cathartic, concealments can be corrosive. Warren is right stating, "the secret is keeping us." Hiding secrets and shame is like swallowing slow-acting poison: one's insides gradually rot. We keep secrets because we long to be loved. We fear what people would think of us if they knew the dust and dirt tucked in our nooks and crannies.

PostSecret became successful because we long to be fully known without being rejected. We want to share our secrets because there is something freeing about being fully open about our inner selves, even anonymously. We long to be free from the fear that we are defined by our dirt.

So, we put up a façade.

The Bible tells the story of a woman who had secrets. We do not know her name, but we know she had been bleeding for twelve years and we know she had kept that a secret because if anyone knew she was bleeding, she would have been shunned. Touching a bleeding woman meant that you became as "unclean" as she was. Yet here she was, in the streets. When near Jesus, she came up behind him and touched his cloak, thinking "If I touch his clothes, I will be healed." Immediately she is healed and freed from her suffering.

When Jesus realizes what has happened, he turns and asks, "Who touched my clothes?"

The disciples were understandably confused and say, "You see the people crowding against you and yet you ask, 'Who touched me?'"

But the woman falls at his feet, trembling, and tells him the whole truth.

Did you get that? She told him the whole truth. Imagine the fear as her confession spilled onto the street. Imagine the feelings as her words dislodged the shame from her soul. Jesus says to her, "Daughter, your faith has healed you. Go in peace and be freed from your suffering" (Mark 5:24–34).

We do not know who this woman was. She is identified by her condition, not her name. She is defined by her secret, not her humanity. But after she reveals the whole truth and is released from her shame, Jesus gives her a new name. He calls her "daughter," a term of endearment and belonging. With one word, he restores her status and bids her to go in peace, healed and restored. Her secret no longer determines her identity.

Shoving away what makes us feel ashamed never works. If doing so gives us relief, it is only temporary.

Instead, we are invited to bring those thoughts and feelings to Christ and talk about them. Say, "Lord, I'm not proud of how this event made me feel or of these thoughts I had, or of what I said here, or did there. Please forgive me and help me." The grip of guilt slowly relaxes and allows us to slip out of the darkness of shame and into the light of forgiveness and grace.

Christ knows our every thought and feeling. He longs for us to surrender our secrets and shame to him so he can take away their power.

In our baptism we are named children of God and promised that no matter what happens, no matter where we go in life, no matter what we do or have done to us, God sees a unique and beloved individual worthy of love, honor, and respect.

The world would like to define us as the daughter who did not mail the Father's Day card, the girl who is hooked on drugs, the man who has lied about his identity since 9/11, or the woman with an eating disorder.

Our secrets do not define us. Our Creator defines us. It would be unwise to start revealing your deepest and darkest secrets to everyone; however, you can tell Jesus. He knows them anyway. He wants you to lay them at his feet, so they no longer have the power to define you.

Like the woman, we are invited to tell Jesus the whole truth—not just the parts that we have rehearsed or prepared, but everything: the good, the bad, the easy, the difficult, the failures and successes, the hopes and disappointments. God wants us to bring everything to him and remember: shame has no place in the kingdom of God.

Even those closest to Jesus knew the sting of shame. In the courtyard outside of Jesus's trial, his disciple Peter denies Jesus. Peter, who was so close to Jesus and pledged his constant loyalty, denies ever knowing Jesus three times. This betrayal comes at Jesus's time of greatest need.

After his heartbreaking threefold denial, the narrative tells us that Peter "wept bitterly" (Matt. 26:75). I cannot imagine.

Yet Peter goes on to become the leader of the first Christian community—the "rock" on which the church was built. That this story is even told at all is a tribute to the candor of the early Christian writers. They did not make the people of the Gospels heroic or super-moral. They shared their truths, warts and all. The disciples were like us: messy, inadequate, and sometimes shameful—yet always, always redeemable.

Many times, I have heard people say they left religion or avoid the church due to feeling judged. Who needs more guilt in their life? But it is important to make some distinctions.

First, *the difference between remorse and repentance*: The apostle Paul says, "For godly grief produces a repentance that leads to salvation and brings no regret, but worldly grief produces death" (2 Cor. 7:10). Worldly grief—remorse—looks at what you have done and produces regret, and regret produces shame. Repentance, on the other hand, is godly grief that drives you to God's grace. Remorse leads you to hate yourself; repentance leads you to hate your sin.

The difference between reprieve and regeneration: When I was younger, I thought I had only so many chances to get myself right with God. In my mind, I would sin, and then I would ask Jesus for forgiveness and Jesus would ask God to give me another chance. Because God loved Jesus, he would grant it. Therefore, I would get a reprieve until I messed up again. It was a terrifying way to live because I never knew when I was going to reach the end of my rope.

Regeneration, on the other hand, understands that what is needed is not another chance, but a change of heart. "Create in me a clean heart, O God" (Ps. 51:10), King David says when he realizes he has done a grievous deed. With regeneration, punishment is not postponed but pardoned and, in response to that great truth, the Holy Spirit regenerates the heart.

The difference between condemnation and conviction. Condemnation leads us to believe we are bad, whereas conviction leads us to understand that we do bad things. Satan loves to suggest our wrongdoings are worthy of punishment. However, the Holy Spirit convicts us of our wrongdoings in order to drive us to the cross. Satan's endgame is to leave us in a shadow of shame; the Holy Spirit's endgame is to bring our wrongdoing into the light in order to correct and forgive.

Is there something in your past you wish were not there? Regrets? Failures? Me too.

Here is the great grace of Jesus: he never leaves you the way he finds you. He did not leave the woman unnamed and unknown. In the same way, he leaves you restored, healed, and renewed. He bids you to give your shame to him and go in peace. Your Creator knows you better than you know yourself—and loves you anyway!

Let me close with a poem I wrote a few years ago. As I was contemplating this whole idea of guilt and shame, these words poured out. Incidents such as my first communion where I got the giggles. I was sure I was going to hell. Communion was sacred and I believed I had defiled it. Then there was the hate I had in my heart for a girl who bullied me at school and was in my youth group at church. Biggest of all was my divorce. Each of these events left me with a great deal of shame. Humiliation hung on my shoulders like an old heavy coat.

And then I met the amazing grace of God. And my remorse turned to repentance. I was convicted, but no longer under the curse of condemnation. The recognition of my sin did not cause me to despair but drove me to the foot of the cross where I was met with grace, forgiveness, and freedom.

The Basement

No, you can't go down there,
See, the steps creak and moan;
And what you may discover
Is best left unknown.

Down there, carefully hidden
In the shadows, I've tucked
All the things I'm ashamed of,
The ugly, the muck.

The words said in anger,
Whole lies and half-truths.
"Shame on you," says my mother,
"And the sins of your youth."

Giggles during the sacred,
The hate in my heart.
"Shame on you," says the pastor,
"Perhaps you don't have a part."

The broken relationships,
The one step too far.
"Shame on you," says myself,
"Can't you see who you are?"

No, don't poke in the shadows,
Please, don't you see?
Waking the monster down there,
Will devour up me!

"But we must," you say,
With your flashlight in hand;
"Don't worry, I'm with you,"
And we slowly descend.

I cringe at what you'll see
With your light, in the glow.
But you gently whisper, "Sweet
child, I already know."

Your beam floods the room,
But nothing's there! Not a trace.
I see now—shame can't survive
In the light of your grace.

For Personal or Group Study:

Thoughts to Consider

- Is it possible your shame will go away if you ignore it?
- What shame have you carried with you? (Only share in a group setting if you feel comfortable. For secrets that are powerful and deep, consider sharing them with a trusted counselor, friend, or clergy.)

- What experiences with shame have you had? Were your parents, coaches, teachers, and others prone to discipline with shame?

- How do you understand the difference between guilt and shame?

- Did your religious background use shame as a motivator to be a "good" Christian?

- How can shame result in anger toward God?

- In your own words, describe the difference between remorse and repentance; reprieve and regeneration; and condemnation and conviction.

Detect the Lie

- If God knew the real me, he would reject me.
- My sin is too deep.
- My shame defines me.
- I know God loves me, but I am pretty sure he is also disappointed in me.
- I am a bad person; I am unredeemable; I cannot change.
- I know God forgives me, but I cannot forgive myself.

Argue against the Lie

- No sin falls outside of God's grace.
- Condemnation, despair, self-degradation, shame, and self-hate have been nailed to the cross.
- One of the godliest attitudes one can have is to respect and love one's self.

- God is not disappointed in you. To believe so is to focus on your sin, not his love.

- Shame was never a part of God's plan; shame has no place in the kingdom of God.

- The Holy Spirit can transform your heart and mind.

Replace the Lie with the Truth (God's Word)

- "There is therefore now no condemnation for those who are in Christ Jesus" (Rom. 8:1).

- "For God did not send his Son into the world to condemn the world, but in order that the world might be saved through him" (John 3:17 ESV).

- "This is how we know what love is: Jesus Christ laid down his life for us" (1 John 3:16 NIV).

- "Distress that drives us to God does that. It turns us around. It gets us back in the way of salvation. We never regret that kind of pain. But those who let distress drive them away from God are full of regrets, end up on a deathbed of regrets" (2 Cor. 7:10 MSG).

- "Instead of your shame you will receive a double portion, and instead of disgrace you will rejoice in your inheritance" (Isa. 61:7 NIV).

- "If we confess our sins, he is faithful and just to forgive us our sins and to cleanse us from all unrighteousness" (1 John 1:9 ESV).

- "I sought the LORD, and he answered me, and delivered me from all my fears. Look to him, and be radiant; so your faces shall never be ashamed" (Ps. 34:4–5).

- "And my people shall never again be put to shame. You shall know that I am in the midst of Israel, and that I, the LORD, am your God and there is no other. And my people shall never again be put to shame" (Joel 2:26).

- "The scripture says, 'No one who believes in him will be put to shame'" (Rom. 10:11).

CHAPTER 8

"Finally, beloved, whatever is true, whatever is honorable, whatever is just, whatever is pure, whatever is pleasing, whatever is commendable, if there is any excellence and if there is anything worthy of praise, think about these things"

(Phil. 4:8).

In her book *Battlefield of the Mind: Winning the Battle in Your Mind,* Christian author and speaker Joyce Meyer talks about the danger of negative thoughts. She asserts you can change your life by changing those destructive thoughts. She says, "If we listen and accept what we hear, the enemy rejoices. If we listen long enough to the deceptive information we have taken in, we will find ourselves facing serious problems."[11] In other words, it is important to think about what we think about.

A proverb from the Bible backs this up: "For as he thinks within himself, so he is" (Prov. 23:7 NASB). The lies we believe about God and about ourselves are like spoiled, rotting food. They stink up and poison all areas of our mind, and therefore, affect our life. Be aware of stinking thinking!

GIGO is a term that was coined when computers were becoming popular. In the early days, not many people were computer-literate, so mistakes were made when it came to programming and productivity. It did not take long to discover a universal truth: if the raw data is bad, the computer cannot do anything good with it. Right data yields right answers and wrong data yields wrong answers. GIGO: Garbage In, Garbage Out.

That maxim is true of the human mind as well. The principle of GIGO applies to our thoughts, and thus our beliefs and actions. If I allow garbage into my mind, it rots my thoughts and attitudes. Sometimes I forget how amazingly influential this thing on top of my neck is.

According to experts who study this type of stuff, the mind thinks between 60,000–80,000 thoughts a day. That is an average of 2,500–3,300 thoughts per hour, which I find incredible.[12] (I wonder how they figure that stuff out. I feel as if I hardly ever complete a thought, and most times my thoughts are mushed together into a big commotion.)

Paul knew the power of our thoughts when he said, "Summing it all up, friends, I'd say you'll do best by filling your minds and meditating on things true, noble, reputable, authentic, compelling, gracious—the best, not the worst; the beautiful, not the ugly; things to praise, not things to curse" (Phil. 4:8 MSG).

Paul was not alone in this advice. Essayist Ralph Waldo Emerson said, "Beware of what you set your mind on because that you surely will become." Minister and author Norman Vincent Peale, who brought the power of positive thinking to the forefront with his best-selling book on that subject, said, "Change your thoughts and you change your world."

Then there is the story about an old Indian Christian who was explaining to a missionary how the battle inside his mind was like a black dog fighting a white dog.

"Which dog wins?" asked the missionary.

"The one I feed the most," replied the Indian.

What are you going to do with the 80,000-some thoughts God has given you today? Which dog are you going to feed? Are you going to allow garbage (Satan's lie) or God's truth to be the focus of your thinking? Positive and negative thoughts cannot live in your mind at the same time. The choice is yours.

Paul warns that even though we may be free to think what we want, it is not always prudent to let our thoughts wander. Everything is permissible, but not everything is beneficial (1 Cor. 6:12). Recently I decided to stop watching late night talk shows. The negative slants and acerbic monologues left me depressed and anxious. The paths my mind went down bothered me and I had to step away.

Chinese philosopher Lao Tzu said: "Watch your thoughts, they become words; watch your words, they become actions; watch your actions, they become habits; watch your habits, they become character; watch your character, it becomes your destiny." Many other famous people have said a version of this truth throughout the years.

A number of years ago, the news reported the story of "Garbage Mary."[13] She lived in a smelly Chicago tenement amid mounds of garbage. She spent her time rummaging through trash cans. She would bum cigarettes off her neighbors. Police took her to a psychiatric hospital and found her to be in a confused state of mind. When they went into her filthy apartment, they were astounded to find stock certificates and bank books indicating she was worth at least a million dollars. Curiously, she was the daughter of a wealthy Illinois lawyer.

This story gives a picture of what happens when we allow garbage to clutter our minds. We have the option of filling our thought life with beautiful treasures, but we let the garbage of this world crowd it out. We surround ourselves with junk when we could immerse ourselves in joy.

Here is the good news. The ability to change our thought life is not left solely up to us. Peale rightly touted the power of positive thinking, but positive thinking only takes us so far. We do have a choice but if we rely only on our efforts, the result becomes about what we can do. True transformation comes from what God can do through us and to us.

Scripture says, "Do not be conformed to this world but be transformed by the renewing of your minds" (Rom. 12:2). Notice you are not told to transform yourself, but to *be* transformed. Your choices are the first step, but the Holy Spirit does the heavy lifting. You need the Holy Spirit to defeat this weapon of deceit. Satan would love nothing more than to keep your thoughts dark, dank, and destructive.

But transformation takes time, so do not beat yourself up if your mind slips into the pit of negativity from time to time. Pick yourself up, dust yourself off, and set your mind back on the path of positivity. Strive for progress rather than perfection.

If you are wondering how to know for certain what is true, noble, reputable, authentic, compelling, gracious, beautiful, and praiseworthy, evangelist D. L. Moody gives a helpful hint: Say you have a stick and you are trying to determine whether it is straight or not. It does no good to argue about whether it is straight. The way to determine whether the stick is straight is to lay it beside another stick that has been determined to be truly straight. The Word of God is the truly straight stick. Lay your thoughts alongside the plumb line of God's truth and see if it holds true. Take every thought captive to Christ to see if it is a thought worth thinking or worth throwing (2 Cor. 10:5). Take your thoughts through The Lie Detector to weed out the worthless and destructive.

To know the truth requires you to know God's Word, which is wisdom (Ps. 19:7). Wisdom does not come from television, the internet, or magazines. It comes from God. The Bible says, "The discerning mind seeks knowledge, but the mouth of fools feeds on folly" (Prov. 15:14 NET). You can either feed on truth or feed on trash. Whatever you fill your mind with is what is going to come out—garbage in, garbage out. If you want to be wise, feed every day on truth, not trash.

Pastor Rick Warren points out three types of "food" with which you can fill your mind: poison, junk food, or health food.[14]

Poison destroys your system. Pornography or overindulgence of alcohol is poison. You may believe you can be around them without consequence, but if that which is profane, blasphemous, evil, vile, and abusive does not bother you, you have a problem. You have become a fool. Be wise. Put on the helmet of salvation. Protect your thoughts.

Junk food is neither good nor bad. It just has no nutritional value at all. Most of the products you see on TV are not evil; they're just junk food. Take when I eat too many Oreo Double Stuf cookies—the more of them I eat, the more I crave the delicious "chunks-o-lard." (That is what my husband calls them.) Yet the calories are empty, and I gain no value from them.

Health food helps you grow and maintain your health. It is truth, and the wise person feeds on truth. It makes you wiser in every area of your life. If you have a steady diet of health food (the truth), it is easier to detect the junk food and poison (the lies).

Fill your mind with God's Word. The more you develop the habit of spending time each day reading and studying the Bible, the wiser you will become.

If we need to know who is true, noble, reputable, authentic, compelling, gracious, beautiful, and praiseworthy, look no further than Christ. Meditate on him, let him take up and take over your thoughts. He guards your heart and mind against the garbage-lies that threaten your peace and identity (Phil. 4:7).

May you feed your mind on the healthiest of diets and may it be in Christ Jesus that your mind is renewed, your thoughts are transformed, and your heart is guarded. It pays to think about what you think about.

For Personal or Group Study:

Thoughts to Consider

- Give an example of how you have experienced or witnessed GIGO.

- Do you believe that what you think about determines who you are?

- In what ways do you feed the dark dog (negative thoughts)?

- In what ways to you feed the white dog (positive thoughts)?

- What kinds of poison or junk food vie for a foothold in your thoughts?

- Is there something/someone in your life that you may need to remove to improve your thought life?

- How do you deal with negativity, especially if it is someone in your family whom you cannot walk away from?

- Can you make a commitment to spend time in God's Word?

Detect the Lie

- My actions are what matter, not my thoughts.

- My circumstances determine my quality of life, not my choices.

- It does not hurt to let a little "garbage" in now and then.

- I cannot control what I think.

- I must think like the world thinks because I live in the world.

Argue against the Lie

- What I think has the power to shape who I am.
- I have a choice about what I think.
- "Stinking thinking" is a weapon of deceit wielded by Satan.
- The Spirit of truth can transform my thoughts.
- God wants us to be transformed people with renewed minds.

Replace the Lie with the Truth (God's Word)

- "As water reflects the face, so one's life reflects the heart" (Prov. 27:19 NIV).

- "Finally, beloved, whatever is true, whatever is honorable, whatever is just, whatever is pure, whatever is pleasing, whatever is commendable, if there is any excellence and if there is anything worthy of praise, think about these things. Keep on doing the things that you have learned and received and heard and seen in me, and the God of peace will be with you" (Phil. 4:8–9).

- "We demolish arguments and every pretension that sets itself up against the knowledge of God, and we take captive every thought to make it obedient to Christ" (2 Cor. 10:5 NIV).

- "Do not be conformed to this world, but be transformed by the renewing of your minds, so that you may discern what is the will of God—what is good and acceptable and perfect" (Rom. 12:2).

- "The thoughts of the righteous are just; the advice of the wicked is treacherous" (Prov. 12:5).

- "Don't become so well-adjusted to your culture that you fit into it without even thinking. Instead, fix your attention on God. You'll be changed from the inside out. Readily recognize what he wants from you, and quickly respond to it. Unlike the culture around you, always dragging you down to its level of immaturity, God brings the best out of you, develops well-formed maturity in you" (Rom. 12:2 MSG).

- "The world is unprincipled. It's dog-eat-dog out there! The world doesn't fight fair. But we don't live or fight our battles that way—never have and never will. The tools of our trade aren't for marketing or manipulation, but they are for demolishing that entire massively corrupt culture. We use our powerful God-tools for smashing warped philosophies, tearing down barriers erected against the truth of God, fitting every loose thought and emotion and impulse into the structure of life shaped by Christ. Our tools are ready at hand for clearing the ground of every obstruction and building lives of obedience into maturity" (2 Cor. 10:3–6 MSG).

CHAPTER 9

ASSUMPTIONS AND PRESUMPTIONS

*"Don't be hypercritical; use your head—and heart!—
to discern what is right, to test what
is authentically right"*

(John 7:24 MSG).

Years after I left my job as the editor-in-chief and founder of a local magazine, one of my former coworkers, Joy, left her job with the company to take a position at another organization. Shortly after she left, a few other former coworkers from the magazine, Tammy and Janet, left to join Joy at her new employer. At first, I was a little miffed. I thought it was rude of Joy to recruit my friends away from the company that still had a special place in my heart.

The next time I talked to Tammy, I expressed my disdain for Joy's behavior. She set me straight. Joy had, in no way, recruited my former coworker. In fact, Joy had discouraged her from making the switch, because she knew Tammy was loyal to the organization and its mission. But Tammy was ready for a change, so she applied for the job and got it. Sure enough, when I talked to Janet, it was a similar story.

Here I was, being all judgy and in a huff when none of what I thought to be true was true. I made an unfortunate—and familiar—mistake. I assumed.

An *assumption* is to suppose something to be true without proof. A *presumption* is to suppose something to be true based on probability. Both are weapons used by the enemy to get us to believe falsehoods about others, ourselves, and God.

The Bible is full of people who made assumptions and presumptions. When Jesus showed up after Lazarus died, his sister Martha said, "Lord, if you had been here, my brother would not have died" (John 11:21). She assumed Jesus did not care; otherwise, he would have hastened his arrival. Rachel, the wife of Jacob, was so distraught about her inability to bear children, she said to her husband, "Give me children, or I shall die!" (Gen. 30:1). She assumed life was only worth living if she could give her husband a son.

God had freed the people of Israel from slavery, but they did not stop complaining. They said, "It is because the Lord hates us that he has brought us out of the land of Egypt to destroy us" (Deut. 1:27). Moses says, "Wait, what?" (that's a paraphrase) and reminds them, "God, your God, is leading the way; he's fighting for you. You saw with your own eyes what he did for you in Egypt; you saw what he did in the wilderness, how God, your God, carried you as a father carries his child, carried you the whole way until you arrived here. But now that you're here, you won't trust God" (Deut. 1:32 MSG).

The Israelites assumed God hated them, and that he was not who he said he was and would not do for them what he said he would do. They bought into the lie that their God had abandoned them—even in the face of much evidence that he had been, and was in fact, still there.

Satan tricks us into making assumptions and presumptions all the time, and it has devastating consequences. I have missed out on wonderful friendships because I assumed the other person did not like me. I have passed on wonderful opportunities because I assumed I was not talented enough. I have been a control freak because I assumed God needed help running my life. The results of my faulty assumptions and presumptions have led to many regrets.

Unfortunately, many people make assumptions about Christianity too. They assume it is for the weak and dull minded. Most of these individuals have never read the Bible, studied doctrine, or even been argued out of believing. They heard someone say that no educated or enlightened person would believe in God, and they assumed that to be true. They took another's word over God's Word and assumed themselves out of believing.

I admire the tax collector Zacchaeus because he made no assumptions. (His story is found in Luke 19.) Jesus had come to town, everyone was curious, and the crowd grew. Zacchaeus was a small man, so he climbed a tree to see Jesus for himself. He did not want to take the crowd's word on who Jesus was. He wanted to see for himself.

As an employee of the Roman government, he was despised by the people gathered there, and people in the crowd made sure Jesus knew Zacchaeus was a crook. Jesus shocked them by inviting himself to dinner at his house.

The crowd is quick to look down their noses at Zacchaeus. This condemnation is sadly the side of Christianity many people experience—the side that is moralistic and self-righteous like the crowd. People who call themselves "saved" yet look down on those deemed "sinners." No wonder people are turned off by religion and say, "No thanks."

Chances are most of us at one time or another have felt judged by someone who claims to know something about the grace of God, but for whom "grace" has become a weapon that belittles people who do not act or believe as they "should." Research by the evangelical polling firm Barna Group finds that young people view churches as "judgmental, overprotective, exclusive and unfriendly toward doubters."[15] Sadly, many people can tell you what the church is against but not for what it is for.

Perhaps too many religious folks buy into "worm theology." Gospel fueled by this belief sounds something like this: "You are worthless and unacceptable to God. There is nothing good in you, but God made you, so he is trying to make the best of it. He gave his Son to die for you and all of God's anger toward you was taken out on Jesus. It's a good thing God is good because you are not."

This theology is called worm theology because the gospel is presented in a way that implies we are all "worms." The church and religious people love to call attention to sin, and then argue over what sin is. Entire blogs, articles, radio shows, and TV programs exist to define sin. Worm theology believes we must convince people of their unworthiness, so they know how much they need the church.

And then there is "wall theology." People who buy into wall theology spend their time figuring out who is "in" and who is "out."

Those on the inside of the wall are saved and those on the outside are not. The church feels it is its duty to bring people inside the wall, so it picks up the megaphone and starts to tell everyone outside the wall about God. Some may be interested, so they come a little closer and, out of curiosity, ask what is going on inside the wall. The church says, "Glad you asked. We're saved, you are not, and we want you to be saved too!"

So, the outsider may say, "OK. What does that mean?" And the religious people, who believe they have it all figured, tell the outsider what one must believe to be rescued. They spout doctrine and creeds. They may say, "Well, first you must believe in the one God who is really three Gods, and then you must be baptized. And just so you know, we sprinkle, not dunk. And we eat and drink Christ's flesh and blood the proper way. If you believe everything we believe, you are one of us!"

And if the outsider is still around by the end of the rant, the church imagines angels doing cartwheels and high fives, saying, "Wonderful! We got another one!"[16]

These two theologies, and many other un-grace-filled ways in which Christians and the church act, make the grace of God look like a country club that exists for the privileged few.

People assume if Christianity were true, it would not produce people who are judgmental and exclusive, so it must be false. We could all learn a lesson from the diminutive Zacchaeus. Get past the crowds and see for yourself what Jesus is all about.

Just how do we do that exactly? Go to the Word of God. Go to the source. Many people discount Christianity because they assume other people's opinions and actions are indicators of Jesus's character.

You cannot assume you know Jesus because you know Christians.

Netflix aired a hit show called *Orange is the New Black.* The story centered around the character Piper Chapman, a privileged white woman who finds herself behind bars in a women's prison. In one episode, Chapman said something that struck me, and I believe it is indicative of what nonbelievers assume about Christianity. Chapman does not believe in God, yet one of her fellow inmates wants her to be baptized. She is about to do it, but then she stops and says she cannot.

She says, "I can't pretend to believe in something I don't, and I don't [believe in this]. I believe in science. I believe in evolution. I believe in Nate Silver and Neil deGrasse Tyson, and Christopher Hutchens. Although I do admit he could be a kind of an asshole. I cannot get behind some supreme being who weighs in on the Tony Awards while a million people get whacked with machetes. I don't believe a billion Indians are going to hell. I don't think we get cancer to learn life lessons, and I don't believe that people die young because God needs another angel. I think it's just bullshit, and, on some level, I think we all know that, I mean, don't you? Look, I understand that religion makes it easier to deal with all of the random shitty things that happen to us. And I wish I could get on that ride, I'm sure I would be happier. But I can't. Feelings aren't enough. I need it to be real."[17]

Ouch. Chapman's rant hurts because it has the ring of truth for many people. She names some of the most common problems people have with God. Maybe deep down, you and I have asked the same questions.

Chapman "needs it to be real." Don't we all need it to be real?

People assume God to be the god Chapman says she cannot believe in. What I wanted to yell at her from the other side of the television screen is that I can understand why she does not believe in that god. I do not believe in that god either!

The God I know is not opposed to science; faith and reason are not exclusive of each other. Christian writer and pastor Dr. Timothy Keller says, "Christianity does not set faith against thinking. It sets faith against assuming."[18]

The God I know does not cause cancer to teach us life lessons. He does not take our loved ones because he needs more angels. That is ridiculous!

The God I know couldn't care less about the Tony Awards, and yes, I am absolutely sure that he hates the fact that people get whacked with machetes.

I would not worship the type of god Chapman describes either.

Pay close attention to how the media portrays Christians. Oftentimes, they are judgmental, clueless, or fanatics. Those portrayals may be the only exposure some people have to a person of faith.

Author Rob Bell, in his book *Love Wins,* says, "Oftentimes when I meet atheists and we talk about the god they don't believe in, we quickly discover that I don't believe in that god either. When we hear that a certain person has 'rejected Christ,' we should first ask, 'Which Christ?'"[19]

Which God would you meet if your assumptions and presumptions about who you think he is crumbled to your feet? What would you find if you met Jesus and not religion?

You would find that Jesus is just as turned off by moral and religious people as you are. When Jesus talks to those who are labeled "sinners," he is gentle and kind. The only times Jesus ever vehemently denounces anyone happen as he lashes out at religious teachers and leaders. The only time he rages occurs against the moralistic and self-righteous people.

After Jesus was crucified, dead, and buried, we find Mary Magdalene, who witnessed the crucifixion, standing outside the tomb of Jesus weeping. "They have taken my Lord away," she says, "and I don't know where they have put him." A man asks her why she is crying and who she is looking for. The man is Jesus, but Mary does not recognize him. She assumes he is the gardener. Only when Jesus calls her name does she recognize her Lord. He is alive and standing right in front of her (John 20:1–18).

Mary almost missed Jesus because she was looking for the wrong Jesus. She assumed his body had been taken away. She presumed his work was over. She assumed his words about his resurrection were nothing more than a fairy tale.

Which Jesus are we looking for? And is he who we suppose him to be?

For Personal or Group Study:

Thoughts to Consider

- Can you think of other people in the Bible who made assumptions about God or about themselves?

- Have you ever taken another person's word about matters of faith and assumed them to be true when they were not?

- Have you ever experienced worm theology? Wall theology?

- Explain how you understand Keller's idea, "Christianity does not set faith against thinking. It sets faith against assuming."

- What clichés have you heard that give the wrong impression of God (example: "God needed another angel in heaven")?

- Can you give some examples of how you have seen Christians portrayed poorly in the media?

Detect the Lie

- I have a good idea about what God is like without reading the Bible.

- My bad experiences with religion and religious people are too hurtful to forget.

- Christianity is exclusive when it maintains Jesus is the only way.

- The church and Christians are a true reflection of who God is.

- I know enough about religion to make up my mind.
- Christianity is for the weak-minded and is a placebo that tries to give people hope.
- God uses guilt to get us to come to church.

Argue against the Lie

- The church is full of hypocrites because the church is full of people.
- Assumptions and presumptions need to be tested against the Word of God for their validity.
- All are unworthy, but no one is worthless.
- Jesus took care of your unworthiness on the cross.
- God alone decides who is "saved" and who is not.
- Other people's opinions and actions are not indicators of who Jesus is.
- You often miss meeting Jesus due to faulty assumptions.
- If you seek God, you will find him.

Replace the Lie with the Truth (God's Word)

- "Keep back your servant also from presumptuous sins; let them not have dominion over me. Then I shall be blameless, and I shall be innocent of great transgression" (Ps. 19:13 ESV).
- "Trust God from the bottom of your heart; don't try to figure out everything on your own. Listen for God's voice in everything you do, everywhere you go; he's the one who

will keep you on track. Don't assume that you know it all" (Prov. 3:5 MSG).

- "We demolish arguments and every pretension that sets itself up against the knowledge of God, and we take captive every thought to make it obedient to Christ" (2 Cor. 10:5 NIV).

- "It is not the healthy who need a doctor, but the sick. I have not come to call the righteous, but sinners" (Mark 2:17 NIV).

- "Don't jump to conclusions—there may be a perfectly good explanation for what you just saw" (Prov. 25:8 MSG).

- "A fool takes no pleasure in understanding, but only in expressing personal opinion" (Prov. 18:2).

- "What marvelous love the Father has extended to us! Just look at it—we're called children of God! That's who we really are. But that's also why the world doesn't recognize us or take us seriously, because it has no idea who he is or what he's up to" (1 John 3:1 MSG).

CHAPTER 10

Knowing about god vs. knowing god

"And this is the real and eternal life: That they know you, the one and only true God, and Jesus Christ, whom you sent"

(John 17:3 MSG).

I love to hear about people's faith journey. Yet, oftentimes when I ask, I hear about how they were raised in the church and what they know about God. I am not interested in what they know *about* God; I want to hear about their walk *with* God. It is the difference between belief and faith. The enemy likes us to confuse the two. He wants us to believe knowing about God is the same as knowing God.

In chapter 7, we read the story of the bleeding woman who reached out and touched Jesus's robe and was healed. One line in that story that has always caused me pause is hearing Jesus say to her, "Daughter, your faith has made you well" (Mark 5:34).

Your faith. What exactly did Jesus mean by that? How much faith is required? Or, for that matter, what is faith?

The writer of Hebrews tells us, "Faith is the assurance of things hoped for, the conviction of things not seen" (Heb. 11:1). I have heard faith compared to traveling down a dark path and only having enough light to see the next step in front of you. Faith allows you to take that next step.

Are faith and belief the same? We often use the words interchangeably. Though they are closely related, they are not the same.

I believe if I eat right and exercise, I will lose weight and feel better. But just because I believe that to be true, I do not necessarily do it. Does that mean I believe it, but do not have faith in it? Does belief inform faith?

When we say the Apostles' Creed, we are saying that we, as Christians, believe certain tenets: "I believe in God the Father. .

. . I believe in Jesus Christ, his only son. . . . I believe in the Holy Spirit. . . . " How is what I profess I believe different from what I profess to have faith in? Perhaps comparing the two will be helpful:

Belief:

- Tends to bring people together.
- Is the basis for a religion.
- Tends to exclude doubt.
- Tries to explain God (creeds and doctrine).

Faith:

- Is an individual thing.
- Is the basis of a relationship.
- Allows for doubt and mystery (accepts that not everything can be explained).
- Wrestles with God.

We could say belief is what we know in our heads and faith is what we know in our hearts. That is not to say that what we know in our hearts is not based on what we know in our heads—there is seeking, questioning, and learning involved in faith—but faith has one more step: reaching out. We reach out toward God in an effort to connect with him—just as the bleeding woman did. She was one in a crowd of people surrounding Jesus. He was pushed against, crowded, and jostled. When Jesus asked the disciples, "Who touched my clothes?" they answered him, "You see the people crowding against you, and yet you can ask, 'Who touched me?'" (Mark 5:30–31). I wonder if they rolled their eyes.

Many people touched him, but only one connected. This act shows us it is possible to be right up against Jesus and still not connect with him.

The same can be said for Philip, one of Jesus's inner circle. Jesus is with him and his other disciples the night he is arrested, and Jesus tells them he is going back to his Father. Philip says, "'Lord, show us the Father, and we will be satisfied.' Jesus said to him, 'Have I been with you all this time, Philip, and you still do not know me?'" (John 14:8–9).

Like Philip, one can be around Jesus for years, listen to his teachings, nod knowingly at his parables, do the work of feeding the hungry and helping the poor—and still miss the point. Philip knew all about Jesus, but he did not know Jesus, and therefore he did not know the Father.

Later, Jesus prays for his friends and for future believers and he says to his Father, "And this is eternal life, that they may know you, the only true God, and Jesus Christ whom you have sent" (John 17:3). Knowing God is not just the point of life, but the definition of life. "This is eternal life, that they may know you."

The Bible says the number-one priority of a Christian is to have a personal relationship with God. Everything else flows from that relationship. Everything else is a consequence. Even faith.

Thirteenth-century philosopher and theologian Thomas Aquinas came up with the concept of three layers of faith. He had fancy Latin names for them: *notia* (knowledge), *assensus* (agreement), and *fiducia* (trust). Let me illustrate how they work in a faith journey.

When I learned that I needed surgery, my doctor recommended a surgeon. I did a little research on this surgeon. I asked others, checked credentials, and examined her experience. I talked to some people she had operated on previously. In other words, I gathered information. That is the first layer of faith: knowledge. Then, from that information, I agreed she was the surgeon for me, which is the second layer of faith: agreement.

Many people have gone through these two layers. They believe in God because they have knowledge of God and affirm it is good to believe in him. It could be likened to brushing their teeth. Parents told them it was a good practice and there is ample evidence to support that claim, so they brush their teeth. We may "practice" faith because it is what was modeled. Our parents went to church, so we go to church. We know facts about God. We believe God exists.

In the book of James, the apostle says, "Do you believe that there is only one God? Good! The demons also believe—and tremble with fear" (James 2:19 GNT).

God bids us to take the crucial and final step of faith—trust. It is the hardest step of the three.

While I knew about and believed in the skills of the surgeon, none of that mattered until I exhibited the trust it took to lie on an operating-room table.

God invites you to move through all three layers of faith by moving from believing things about him to believing him. There is a difference. One reason trust may be so difficult is it requires us to be vulnerable. Lying unconscious on the operating table surrounded by people with scalpels is a vulnerable place to be.

Have you ever experienced a trust fall? You stand in front of a person and fall back into his or her arms, trusting you will be caught. Everything in your head tells you not to do it. You may know the person can catch you. You agree he or she will catch you.

However, you do not exhibit trust until you lean back—without moving your feet—and actually fall backward.

You can say, "I know God is the Creator. I know Jesus is the Savior." You can run through the whole list of doctrinal truths and creeds—but unless you fall back into his arms, you have not taken the last and necessary step of faith that fosters a relationship that transforms your heart. Vulnerability paves the way to becoming a new creation.

Jesus came to have a transformational relationship with you—"to make all things new" (Rev. 21:5). In the movie *The Passion of the Christ,* Mary sees her son Jesus fall under the weight of his cross. She remembers running to him when he fell as a child and despite the crowd and his captors, she races to him now. Raising her son's beaten and bruised face from the earth, she says, "I am here." Jesus sees her, and responds, "See, Mother, I make all things new."[20]

That line gives me goosebumps every time. The only way all things can be made new is because Christ walked the road to death. The old world of alienation and death is reclaimed by God through Christ to be a new world of reconciliation and life. Jesus was "life, and the life was the light of all people" (John 1:4). Death tried to hold him down; darkness tried to finish him off—but darkness could not overcome light, and death could not hold down life.

The act of trust throws you into the transformational truth of Jesus's lordship. That is what biblical faith is: falling into the arms of Jesus.

How do we know we will be caught?

We believe the truth. We do not only believe things about God; we believe God says what he means, does what he promises, and will never change.

Psalm 62:11–12 (NIV) says, "One thing God has spoken, two things I have heard: 'Power belongs to you, God, and with you, Lord, is unfailing love.'" In other words: God is power, and God is unfailing love. If he was loving but not powerful, he wouldn't be very effective. If he were all-powerful but not loving, we would be in trouble. He is perfectly both. Can you trust a God like that with your life? Can you let a God like that be the boss of you? Can you trust a God like that to catch you when you fall?

All my life I have known about God. I went to Sunday School, Vacation Bible School, camps, and confirmation. I memorized Martin Luther's Small Catechism and Bible verses, but as sometimes happens, in my adult life things fell apart. And so did I. I was not sure how I was going to survive. In my desperation, I opened up to the Jesus I knew about but did not know. When I was at a loss for what to do, I came back to a God I had heard say he loved me. And it saved my life.

The bleeding woman had gone to all kinds of doctors looking for a cure. We too look to all kinds of "doctors" to offer us a cure—to give us contentment—to create meaning. Maybe our doctor is prosperity or popularity or perfectionism or piety.

When we understand that Jesus is the only cure, then we are able to move from a set of beliefs about him to faith in him. We move from a religion to a relationship.

Yet, we may still wonder how much faith is enough. Is there a quantifier to our faith? You hear people say, "She's a woman of great faith" or "His faith has grown stronger."

I have always thought the bleeding woman's faith must have been rock-solid, but I have become convinced that it is the direction of her faith that matters, not the depth of it.

Take terrorists, for example. They strap explosives to their bodies and blow themselves up in the middle of crowds of innocent people. That extreme behavior must take a tremendous depth of faith. Consider cults where hundreds of people drink poisoned Kool-Aid at the command of a crazy leader. People in these situations must have had a faith that was strong, but terribly misdirected. It is the direction, not the depth, of faith that matters.

Look at it this way: three people are in a burning apartment building and the only escape is to jump from a six-story window to the firefighters' tarp below. The firefighters promise to catch each of them. The first person jumps with confidence and is saved. The second tenant is not so sure and jumps with some hesitation. He is saved. The third person is scared to death. He is highly doubtful that this act of jumping is a good idea, but he does it, screaming "I'm gonna die!" all the way down. He, too, is saved.

Which of these three men are more "saved?" The one who had complete and total trust in the firefighters or the one who yelled all the way down?

They were all saved—not because of the amount of their faith in the firefighters, but because they jumped. How much faith do you have to have to be saved? Just enough to leap.

I find this assurance wonderfully comforting. I am not saved by my faith; I am saved through my faith. It is the object of my faith that counts. Quantity of faith does not matter; placement of faith does.

Jesus did not say, "Believe certain things about me." He said, "Believe in God, believe also in me" (John 14:1).

Satan would have you believe that knowing about Jesus is enough. But that thinking will never transform your heart. If you believe in Jesus but do not feel as if you know Jesus, and you want to know him, just tell him: "Lord, I know all about you, but I want to know you. Give me the courage to jump; the courage to reach out; the courage to connect."

Here is more good news. It is not our job to conjure up faith—it is the job of the Holy Spirit. The reformer Martin Luther says, "I believe that by my own understanding or strength I cannot believe in Jesus Christ my Lord or come to him, but instead the Holy Spirit has called me through the gospel."[21]

The transforming nature of God's Spirit keeps us in the true faith by making him the object of our faith. God is the only doctor who can meet your needs. He may not give us better life circumstances, but he will give us himself, which is what we really need.

One last question: Does the Lord want us to trust God or to please God? When we try to please God, the focus becomes our efforts, lists of dos and don'ts. Our focus is turned to our attitudes and behaviors. When we trust the Lord, the focus shifts to God's grace and love. We acknowledge that our actions are not always appropriate but count on God to shape us through our mistakes and shortcomings. Success is engaging in the journey and depending on God to get us where we need to go. Asking whether we are pleasing God is the wrong question. The right question is, "Do we trust him?"

For Personal or Group Study:

Thoughts to Consider

- How would you describe the difference between belief and faith?

- What do you believe without a doubt?

- Who or what do you have faith in?

- Can you see the three layers of faith in your life?

- Do you wish you had stronger faith?

- When you hear "it is the object of your faith that counts, not the depth of it," how does that affect you?

- How hard is it for you to trust someone? Do they have to earn your trust first or do you trust them until they lose it?

- What kind of "doctors" do you or others seek to look for a "cure"?

- Do you know about God, or do you feel you know God?

Detect the Lie

- God is not trustworthy. (He is not who he says he is.)

- I can find my own "cure" for what ails me.

- If I have doubts, my faith is lacking.

- Knowing about God and Jesus, and believing they exist, is enough.

- Religion is the same as a relationship.

- I am in trouble because my faith is weak and fluctuating.

- It is up to me to conjure faith.

Argue against the Lie:

- The object of our faith is what matters, not the amount of it.

- Creeds, rituals, and traditions help us express our faith but are not a substitute for it.

- Doubt does not indicate a weak faith; rather, it is a part of faith.

- What/who you have faith in is far more important than how much faith you have.

- God is faithful, even when we are not.

- God is both all-powerful and all-loving.

- The Holy Spirit awakens faith within us.

Replace the Lie with the Truth (God's Word)

- "Now this is eternal life: that they know you, the only true God, and Jesus Christ, whom you have sent" (John 17:3 NIV).

- "Do not let your hearts be troubled. Believe in God, believe also in me" (John 14:1).

- "The fundamental fact of existence is that this trust in God, this faith, is the firm foundation under everything that makes life worth living. It's our handle on what we can't see" (Heb. 11:1–2 MSG).

- "Blessed are those who trust in the LORD, whose trust is the LORD. They shall be like a tree planted by water, sending out its roots by the stream. It shall not fear when heat comes, and its leaves shall stay green; in the year of drought it is not anxious, and it does not cease to bear fruit" (Jer. 17:7–8).

- "So let God work his will in you. Yell a loud no to the Devil and watch him make himself scarce. Say a quiet yes to God and he'll be there in no time" (James 4:7 MSG).

- "May the God of hope fill you with all joy and peace in believing, so that you may abound in hope by the power of the Holy Spirit" (Rom. 15:13 MSG).

- "Our soul waits for the LORD; he is our help and shield. Our heart is glad in him, because we trust in his holy name" (Ps. 33:20).

- "If we are faithless, he remains faithful—for he cannot deny himself" (2 Tim. 2:13).

- "Jesus, overhearing, shot back, 'Who needs a doctor: the healthy or the sick? Go figure out what this Scripture means: "I'm after mercy, not religion." I'm here to invite outsiders, not coddle insiders'" (Matt. 9:13 MSG).

- "'If you can?' said Jesus. 'Everything is possible for one who believes.' Immediately the boy's father exclaimed, 'I do believe; help me overcome my unbelief!'" (Mark 9:23–24 NIV).

- "No one can say 'Jesus is Lord' except by the Holy Spirit" (2 Cor. 12:3).

- "When the Advocate [Holy Spirit] comes, whom I will send to you from the Father, the Spirit of truth who comes from the Father, he will testify on my behalf" (John 15:26).

CHAPTER 11

"Blessed are those who hunger and thirst for righteousness, for they shall be satisfied"

(Matt. 5:6).

ontentment. Isn't that a beautiful word? Sit in it for a while. Let it wash over you. Wrap it around your shoulders. When was the last time you felt content?

Unfortunately, Satan uses the promise of contentment like a carrot on a stick. In the lie that God is not who he says he is, the enemy invites us to look for satisfaction outside of God's providence. We race after it, desire it, taste it here and there, but our hearts are more like black holes than sponges—never satiated, never satisfied for long. We search in shallow wells and pant over dried ponds.

King David makes a better suggestion: "As a deer longs for flowing streams, so my soul longs for you, O God" (Ps. 42:1). The only water that will quench our thirst is from the well that is God.

Putting our hope for contentment in the world is like putting our hope in the elusive Wizard of Oz. Behind his curtained façade, he makes promises he does not have the power to grant. He swears to fulfill our wishes if we do the work. Even if we do the work, when the curtain is pulled back, we are disappointed, angry, and most certainly disillusioned.

One word sums up our dilemma: "anticippointment"—a term coined by a 1960s ad agency as a holiday card punchline. Have you ever anticipated an event or a holiday with great excitement, only to be disappointed in the outcome?

My sister Roxie, who passed away in 1993, was the queen of anticippointment. She was full of life, always quick with a joke, followed by her infectious laugh. She looked forward to every holiday, birthday, and vacation with such anticipation, but these events never lived up to her expectations.

Perhaps we have all experienced unmet expectations. I was really looking forward to treating myself to one of those salt flotation spas. You spend an hour in a tub full of room-temperature water salty enough to keep you afloat. The room is dark and basically, you just lie there. Because of sensory deprivation, this therapy is supposed to help you unwind. The website says, "Your senses get a break from the large amount of input that we experience in everyday life" which may result in "relief from the stresses of everyday life, improved creativity and athletic performance." Who would not want that? So I gave it a try.

The experience was wonderful. Sorta. You see, I was so busy trying to "do it right" I ruined it. I kept thinking, "Am I in the right position? Wait, am I sure all my muscles are relaxed? Why can't I relax my muscles? Aren't I supposed to be experiencing some kind of epiphany? I heard people sometimes experience epiphanies in these types of baths. What if I wasted my money? I need to stop thinking. How do I stop thinking? Stop thinking!"

Can you see my dilemma? I had all these expectations—even though I told myself to go in without any—but I just could not help it. Instead of relaxing in the embrace of the water and enjoying a state of "being," I could not quit worrying if I were "doing" it right. I felt it was somehow up to me to make this experience worthwhile instead of just trusting it to work. I failed to trust the process. I was *anticippointed*.

I tend to do that. I have trouble just "being." The same happens with grace. To experience grace correctly, I believe I must be doing, earning, gaining. Why can't I just relax in the arms of Jesus and let his love wash over me and keep me afloat? I think it is a human tendency to make grace something we must earn; something that depends on us. "Am I doing it right? What if I am not? Is God disappointed in me? What about other people? Are they experiencing grace? How are they experiencing it? Should I be doing more? Stop thinking!"

We all have expectations of ourselves and of others. Where does our hope for contentment lie? We may place our hope in other people. One of the red flags that pops up during premarital counseling happens when the couple says they make each other happy. While it may be true that they bring out the best in one another, if one relies on the other one to make him or her happy, chances are good that disappointment will be for supper.

I guarantee that our spouses, children, friends, and coworkers will let us down. And I can guarantee you that I have let my husband, children, friends, and coworkers down at one time or another. Because I am human.

Perhaps we put our hope in earthly treasures such as wealth, possessions, status, looks, or approval. Whatever it is we think we must own, owning it may satisfy for a while, but soon we want the next best gadget. The prizes of this world are as tenuous as shifting sand at a beach volleyball tournament.

Perhaps we put our hope in ourselves. We hold ourselves to certain standards of behavior or achievements. We get out the measuring stick and hold it up to others and to ourselves and neither ever seems to measure up.

If you put your hope in the government, you will be disappointed. If you put your hope in the church, you will be disappointed. If you say, "I will be happier when I secure a new job . . . lose weight . . . find a spouse . . . get a new spouse"—whatever it may be—you will be disappointed.

A nursery rhyme says it best, "The bear went over the mountain, the bear went over the mountain, the bear went over the mountain, to see what he could see. And all that he could see, and all that he could see, was the other side of the mountain, the other side of the mountain, was all that he could see."

I am sure he was disappointed.

God offers a solution. Listen to his summons: "Hey there! All who are thirsty, come to the water! Are you penniless? Come anyway—buy and eat! Come, buy your drinks, buy wine and milk. Buy without money—everything's free! Why do you spend your money on junk food, your hard-earned cash on cotton candy? Listen to me, listen well: eat only the best, fill yourself with only the finest" (Isa. 55:1–2 MSG).

What an invitation! Just as we would starve physically without daily bread and water, nourishment is also necessary for our souls. This scripture reminds us that nourishment is freely offered, and asks an important question: Why do we spend time and money on so much that offers no contentment—like junk food for the soul?

The solution to our anticippointment in life is to quit believing the lie that the world can deliver what we think we need. Jesus says that relying on anything other than his truth is like one "who built his house on sand" (Matt. 7:26–27).

On Christ the solid rock we stand. When everything else is fleeting and disappointing, we know the promises made to us in God's Word transcends them all and God is who he says he is.

C. S. Lewis was a brilliant Christian writer and thinker. He was an atheist until the age of thirty-three, and one of the main reasons he was led to Christianity was his anticippointment with life. He longed for something this world could neither satisfy nor adequately answer.

David Mathis, executive editor of DesiringGod.org, says of Lewis: "He had learned all too well that relentless rationality could not adequately explain the depth and complexity of human life, or the textures and hues of the world in which we find ourselves. From early on, an angst gnawed at him which one day he would express so memorably in his most well-known single book, *Mere Christianity:* 'If I find in myself a desire which no experience in this world can satisfy, the most probable explanation is that I was made for another world.'"[22]

We were meant for more than what this world can give. Perhaps our expectations are too high. Actually, it is the opposite. Listen again to Lewis: "If we consider the unblushing promises of reward and the staggering nature of the rewards promised in the Gospels, it would seem that our Lord finds our desires not too strong, but too weak. We are half-hearted creatures, fooling about with drink and sex and ambition when infinite joy is offered us, like an ignorant child who wants to go on making mud pies in a slum because he cannot imagine what is meant by the offer of a holiday at the sea. We are far too easily pleased."[23]

Did you get that? "We are far too easily pleased." What the world offers is nothing compared to the promises we have in Christ. Those promises make a difference in our lives now. My guess is that you do not want to live on some faraway promise of contentment in the afterlife. You need the strength to get through today. And even if you are fortunate enough to have a life filled with comfort today, you desire more and hope life has a purpose beyond being comfortable.

Jesus said the kingdom of God is now—you can have freedom, joy, peace, and contentment *now* (Luke 17:21).

I am writing this book because Christ has changed my life in the present, and I want that for you. I want you to have the freedom that comes from being able to forgive and be forgiven. I want you to know the peace that passes all understanding that Christ has made available to us now (Phil. 4:7). I want to share with you the contentment that comes from having a relationship with your Redeemer. I want you to know the joy of living a life with purpose today.

I am not saying I have all of this figured out—I am still a work in progress and always will be this side of heaven. But when I start looking for contentment in the wrong places, I remember these four words from writer and pastor Dr. Timothy Keller: Rely, Obey, Relax, and Expect.[24]

Rely: It is a question to ask continually: "On what, or whom, am I relying?" Nothing in our lives should give us more hope, more satisfaction, or more meaning than God.

Obey: Obedience isn't just a change of behavior; it is a change of heart. It's about uprooting the lie. It is not about trying to be a better person but being transformed into a different person. If you rely on God to define who you are, then you obey him because you want to, not because you feel you are supposed to. The motivation for obedience is dedication, not obligation.

Relax: Relaxing is hard for me because I like control and because I am used to having to work for what I want. But we can relax in the arms of God's saving grace through Jesus Christ. Christ says to trust in what he has done, not in what you can do.

Expect: Remember, the one who loves you more than you can imagine is also the One who holds the universe in his hands. The power of the Spirit that rose Jesus from the dead is the same power that lives in you. Paul says, "God can do anything, you know— far more than you could ever imagine or guess or request in your wildest dreams!" (Eph. 3:20 MSG).

God invites us to not be so easily pleased. The world is full of shiny glittery promises that, when grasped, turn out to be tarnished and temporary. Turn your eyes away from empty promises and false façades, and discover more than you hoped for in Christ.

For Personal or Group Study:

Thoughts to Consider

- What does contentment look like to you?
- When was the last time you were content? Are you now?
- If you are not content, what is it you lack?
- Have you ever experienced anticippointment?
- Have you ever relied on another person or possession to make you happy?
- How have you been far too easily pleased?
- Which is harder for you: rely, obey, relax, or expect?

Detect the Lie

- Treasures of this world will satisfy me.
- I will be happy when I have all I want.
- If I do not have everything I want, there must be something wrong with me.
- If I am not content, it is God's fault.
- If God really loved me, he would make sure I am happy and comfortable.

Argue against the Lie

- True contentment is found in the promises of God through Christ.

- Not every need or want will be met on my timetable or my terms.
- No matter the circumstances, I can trust all is well with my soul.
- The kingdom of God is at hand; contentment and peace are available to me now.

Replace the Lie with the Truth (God's Word)

- "The Lord will guide you continually, and satisfy your needs in parched places, and make your bones strong; and you shall be like a watered garden, like a spring of water, whose waters never fail" (Isa. 58:11).
- "But godliness with contentment is great gain" (1 Tim. 6:6 NIV).
- "Keep your lives free from the love of money, and be content with what you have; for he has said, 'I will never leave you or forsake you'" (Heb. 13:5).
- "But he said to me, 'My grace is sufficient for you, for power is made perfect in weakness.' So, I will boast all the more gladly of my weaknesses, so that the power of Christ may dwell in me. Therefore I am content with weaknesses, insults, hardships, persecutions, and calamities for the sake of Christ; for whenever I am weak, then I am strong" (2 Cor. 12:9–10).
- "I [Paul] am not saying this because I am in need, for I have learned to be content whatever the circumstances. I know what it is to be in need, and I know what it is to have plenty. I have learned the secret of being content in any

and every situation, whether well fed or hungry, whether living in plenty or in want. I can do all this through him who gives me strength" (Phil. 4:11–13 NIV).

- "Delight yourself in the LORD, and he will give you the desires of your heart" (Ps. 37:4 ESV).

- "Don't look for shortcuts to God. The market is flooded with surefire, easygoing formulas for a successful life that can be practiced in your spare time. Don't fall for that stuff, even though crowds of people do. The way to life—to God!—is vigorous and requires total attention" (Matt. 7:13–14 MSG).

- "Let them thank the LORD for his steadfast love, for his wonderful works to humankind. For he satisfies the thirsty, and the hungry he fills with good things" (Ps. 107:8–9).

- "I will fully satisfy the weary, and all who are faint I will replenish" (Jer. 31:25).

- "Blessed are those who hunger and thirst for righteousness, for they shall be satisfied" (Matt. 5:6 ESV).

- "Jesus said to them, 'I am the bread of life. Whoever comes to me will never be hungry, and whoever believes in me will never be thirsty'" (John 6:35).

- "The poor shall eat and be satisfied; those who seek him shall praise the LORD. May your hearts live forever!" (Ps. 22:26).

CHAPTER 12

"Peace I leave with you; my peace I give to you. I do not give to you as the world gives. Do not let your hearts be troubled, and do not let them be afraid"

(John 14:27).

Perhaps you have read some of the bloopers that have found their way into church bulletins and newsletters:

- This afternoon there will be a meeting in the South and North ends of the church. Children will be baptized at both ends.

- The Reverend Merriweather spoke briefly, much to the delight of the audience.

- Eight new choir robes are currently needed, due to the addition of several new members and to the deterioration of some of the older ones.

And this one:

- Don't let worry kill you—let the church help.

Hopefully, your church is not killing you with worry. Anxiety and worry result from believing the lie that God does not have our best interests in mind. It is not too much to say all lies lead to sin, and worry is a sin. This statement is not to minimize the seriousness of anxiety disorders. I am referring to those of us who have a choice but allow worry and fret to steal our peace. Satan loves it when we wring our hands and occupy our minds with worry.

What do we worry about? Perhaps the better question would be, what don't we worry about? Worrying has the potential to suck the life out of us. No wonder the word "worry" originates from words that mean "to strangle." Worry chokes out the life-giving hope and joy—the abundant life—Jesus said he came to give.

In our anxiousness, we convince ourselves that if what we are worried about happened, it would be awful. Yet, most of what we stress about is highly unlikely to happen. Chances are, if it did happen, it may not be pleasant, but it probably would not be as horrible as we anticipate. It is our human tendency to "catastrophize."

Jesus must have known our propensity to worry. He asks, "Can any one of you by worrying add a single hour to your life?" (Matt. 6:27 NIV). Yet we can't help ourselves, so we become like the not-so-superhero "Anxiety Annie"—able to jump to the worst conclusion in a single bound.

Here is an example of how I "catastrophize." The other day I had a pain in my side. "Oh great," I immediately thought, "My cancer has returned." Or perhaps my friends or coworkers seem distant; I wonder what I did to offend them. When either of my sons missed a curfew in high school, within five minutes I imagined him lying in a ditch. A bit dramatic, I know. Please tell me I am not alone.

Our lives are full of terrible misfortune—most of which never happened. One study affirms this thought, concluding 85 percent of what we worry about never happens. Within the 15 percent that did happen, seventy-nine percent of the subjects discovered they could handle the difficulty better than expected or were taught a lesson they thought was worth learning.[25] This research concludes that 97 percent of what one worries about is a futile exercise in exaggerations and misperceptions.

You may wonder (or worry) about the 3 percent representing legitimate worries. Aren't there situations about which we should be genuinely concerned? Yes, but all is not lost, because there is a difference between worry and concern.

Worry is ruminating over something without making any progress toward a solution. Dictionaries support this idea with definitions such as "to touch or disturb something repeatedly," or "to subject to persistent or nagging attention or effort."[26] Worry can be understood as hand-wringing that tends to focus on the future. American writer Jodi Picoult said, "[Worry] is like a rocking chair. It gives you something to do but it doesn't get you very far."

Concern, on the other hand, is solution oriented. It focuses on solving the problem, not going over the same points again and again without adding any value to the situation. Concern is thinking of options, setting priorities, and drawing conclusions. It focuses on the present and works to solve the problem.

Worry is meditating on "what if?" Concern is meditating on "what is?"

To help us determine the difference between "what if" and "what is," this diagram divides the events of life into three areas:
1) what we can control;
2) what we can influence;
3) what is out of our control or influence.

If you have control, you can act with concern by making a plan and working toward a solution.

If you have influence, you can take indirect action to sway the outcome.

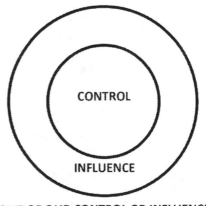

CONTROL

INFLUENCE

OUT OF OUR CONTROL OR INFLUENCE

If the circumstance is out of your control or influence, you have a choice: worry or trust God.

Examples of what we can control:

- Our attitude
- The way we respond to people and circumstances
- Choices we make (examples: what we eat, what we wear, where we go)

Examples of what we can influence:

- Our loved ones
- People we interact with: strangers, acquaintances, coworkers
- Government (by our vote)
- Our health (to a certain extent by exercise and diet)

Examples of what is not in our control or influence:

- The weather
- The stock market/economy
- Our health (to a certain extent)
- Randomness of the universe (how is that for a catch-all category?)

You get the idea. It is sobering to think about how little we ultimately control. The way to cope and find peace in this dangerous world is to relinquish all worries to God through prayer. Unfortunately, prayer is often thought of as a last resort when God invites us to make it the first resort.

This diagram illustrates how all roads lead to banishing worry:

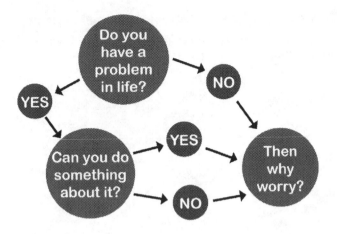

In a way, this diagram might seem too simplistic—and it is. Worry is complex and addictive. None of us wake up in the morning thinking, "I want to worry today." Yet it plagues our society. If we scratch below the surface of worry, we expose the real culprit: fear. Fear births worry. Jesus knew our propensity to be afraid, so he gave us these assurances:

- When Jesus's friends witnessed his transfiguration before them, where his face shone like the sun and his clothes became dazzling white, they were terrified. But Jesus came and touched them, saying, "Get up and do not be afraid" (Matt. 17:7).

- Jesus said to the leader of the synagogue whose daughter was ill, "Do not be afraid; only believe" (Mark 5:36).

- When Jesus called Simon to a career change, he said, "Do not be afraid; from now on you will be catching people" (Luke 5:10).

- Just before Jesus left his friends and went back to his Father in heaven, he said, "Do not let your hearts be troubled, and do not let them be afraid" (John 14:27).

- When Paul was preaching to people who reviled him, the Lord said to him in a vision, "Do not be afraid" (Acts 18:9).

According to some Bible scholars, Jesus or God says, "do not fear," or "do not be afraid," 365 times—one assurance for every day of the year.

Which of these fears speaks to you?

- Loss of control
- Loss of love
- Loss of a loved one
- Loss of health
- Loss of security
- Death
- Lack of physical comfort
- Loss of money
- What others may think of me
- What God may think of me
- What else?

The disciples were no strangers to fear. One well-known story took place in a boat tossed and turned by a violent storm. They were out on the water when a great windstorm hit, and the boat was swamped with water. Jesus, surprisingly, was asleep on a cushion in the back of the boat. The disciples woke him up saying,

"Don't you care that we are perishing?" Jesus rebukes the storm and the waters become dead calm. He looked at his friends and asked, "Why are you afraid?"

They were amazed, their eyes widened, and they said amongst themselves, "Who then is this, that even the wind and the sea obey him?" (Mark 4:35–41).

I am always struck by their question to Jesus, "Don't you care that we are perishing?" Our fear often comes from believing God does not care that the world is tossed and turned by violence and uncertainty. Doesn't he care that we are perishing? Doesn't he notice how hard we are trying to keep our heads above water?

Dr. David Lose, senior pastor at Mount Olivet Lutheran Church in Minneapolis, Minnesota, asks the question on his blog, DavidLose.net: "What moves us from fear to faith?"

Fear and faith are similar in that each are concerned with something unknown. Each may be challenging, even threatening. Each present a choice to be made, but rarely is it an either/or option. Faith does not so much replace fear as it makes it possible to cope with fear.

We may assert it would be easier for us to cope with fear if we just had a miracle or two to convince us God really is who he says he is. Yet that is exactly what the disciples experience—a miracle. It does not seem to expel the fear but shifts the fear and they proclaim with astonishment, "Who is this man?" Even after all they had witnessed Jesus do, they were still unsure of who Jesus was.

Lose writes: "The shift in the disciples' reaction—from 'do you not care we are perishing' to 'who is this'—signifies a shift from what, the miracle, to who, Jesus. Which leads me to conclude that perhaps the answer to our question—'What moves us from fear to faith?'—is a relationship. It's the move from what to who, from event to person, from ambiguous miracle to the actual person of Jesus."[27]

The faith we need to help us cope with fear is not found in a diagram on worry (as helpful as that may be) or in an in-depth study of theology, or even in our effort to try harder. Rather, faith is about a relationship with the God revealed by the actions and words of Jesus.

There is a children's blessing that states, "God is good, all the time; all the time, God is good." If we do not believe this to be true, worry and fear will be our companions. If we believe this fact is true, trust and assurance will be our companion, for we know our God always has our best interests in mind, even if it feels as if the waves are winning. Evangelist Oswald Chambers said,

> Fill your mind with the thought that God is there. And once your mind is truly filled with that thought, when you experience difficulties it will be as easy as breathing for you to remember, "My heavenly Father knows all about this!" Jesus said there are times when God cannot lift the darkness from you, but you should trust him. At times God will appear like an unkind friend, but he is not; he will appear like an unnatural father, but he is not; he will appear like an unjust judge, but he is not. Keep the thought that the mind of God is behind all things strong and growing. Not even the smallest detail of life happens unless God's will is behind it. Therefore, you can rest in perfect confidence in him.[28]

The enemy will try to convince us God does not care that we are perishing. Jesus tells us we will have troubles in this world but to take heart—he has overcome the world (John 16:33).

When I discovered I had cancer, I was blessed that surgery took care of the disease before it had spread. By the time I found out I had cancer, I was already cancer-free. I praised the Lord, saying, "God is good, all the time!" But what if the cancer had spread? What if it had not been caught in time? I hope I would still praise the Lord, saying, "God is good, all the time." Because he is. Even when circumstances are not OK, they are OK. I am God's beloved daughter and not even death can take that away from me.

In the hymn "A Mighty Fortress is Our God" Reformer Martin Luther reminds us that God's truth triumphs:

> And though this world, with devils filled,
> Should threaten to undo us,
> We will not fear, for God hath willed
> His truth to triumph through us.
> The Prince of Darkness grim,—
> We tremble not for him;
> His rage we can endure,
> For lo! His doom is sure,—
> One little word shall fell him.
>
> That word above all earthly powers—
> No thanks to them—abideth;
> The Spirit and the gifts are ours
> Through him who with us sideth.

Let goods and kindred go,

This mortal life also:

The body they may kill:

God's truth abideth still,

His kingdom is for ever.[29]

For Personal or Group Study:

Thoughts to Consider

- Do you believe God has your best interests in mind?
- Are you like Anxiety Girl—jumping to the worst conclusion in a single bound?
- Can you think of a time when you "catastrophized" a situation?
- Can you give an example of the difference between worry and concern?
- Do you view prayer as a last resort?
- How comfortable are you when you are not in control?
- Which fear(s) listed speaks to you the loudest?
- Do you sometimes feel as if God does not care that you are perishing?

Detect the Lie

- I must have control over my life, or everything will go wrong.
- I know what right looks like.
- It is loving to worry about my loved ones.

- God created the world out of nothing and set all affairs in order, but I am not quite sure he knows how to run my week.
- If plans do not go as desired, the result will be terrible.
- God may be good, but that does not mean he will be good to me.

Argue against the Lie

- Nothing I am worried about is out of God's control.
- I can trust God with my and my loved ones' circumstances.
- If something terrible goes wrong, I can handle it with God's help.
- Even if it is not OK, I will be OK.
- What I am worried about is unlikely to happen anyway.
- Prayer is the first resort, not the last.
- Concern is helpful; worry is a thief.

Replace the Lie with the Truth (God's Word)

- "Don't fret or worry. Instead of worrying, pray. Let petitions and praises shape your worries into prayers, letting God know your concerns. Before you know it, a sense of God's wholeness, everything coming together for good, will come and settle you down. It's wonderful what happens when Christ displaces worry at the center of your life" (Phil. 4:6–7 MSG).
- "I keep my eyes always on the Lord. With him at my right hand, I will not be shaken" (Ps. 16:8 NIV).

- "I lift up my eyes to the hills—from where will my help come? My help comes from the Lord, who made heaven and earth" (Ps. 121:1–2).

- "Don't fuss about what's on the table at mealtimes or if the clothes in your closet are in fashion. There is far more to your inner life than the food you put in your stomach, more to your outer appearance than the clothes you hang on your body. Look at the ravens, free and unfettered, not tied down to a job description, carefree in the care of God. And you count far more.

  "Has anyone by fussing before the mirror ever gotten taller by so much as an inch? If fussing can't even do that, why fuss at all? Walk into the fields and look at the wildflowers. They don't fuss with their appearance—but have you ever seen color and design quite like it? The ten best-dressed men and women in the country look shabby alongside them. If God gives such attention to the wildflowers, most of them never even seen, don't you think he'll attend to you, take pride in you, do his best for you?

  "What I'm trying to do here is get you to relax, not be so preoccupied with getting so you can respond to God's giving. People who don't know God and the way he works fuss over these things, but you know both God and how he works. Steep yourself in God-reality, God-initiative, God-provisions. You'll find all your everyday human concerns will be met. Don't be afraid of missing out. You're my dearest friends! The Father wants to give you the very kingdom itself" (Luke 12:22–32 MSG).

- "Peace I leave with you; my peace I give you. I do not give to you as the world gives. Do not let your hearts be troubled and do not be afraid" (John 14:27).

- "Pile your troubles on God's shoulders—he'll carry your load, he'll help you out" (Ps. 55:22 MSG).

- "Cast all your anxiety on him, because he cares for you" (2 Pet. 5:7).

- "Trust in the Lord with all your heart, and do not rely on your own insight" (Prov. 3:5).

- "God is our refuge and strength, a very present help in trouble. Therefore we will not fear, though the earth should change, though the mountains shake in the heart of the sea; though its waters roar and foam, though the mountains tremble with its tumult" (Ps. 46:1–3).

CHAPTER 13

"So I tell you, whatever you ask for in prayer, believe that you have received it, and it will be yours"

(Mark 11:24).

ittle Suzy came home from school and went straight to her room and started to pray out load. Her mom, who was working in the kitchen, heard her saying, "London, London, London," very loudly.

Opening the door to her bedroom she asked, "What are you doing?" She replied, "I'm praying." Her mom asked, "What does 'London' have to do with your prayers?" Suzy said, "I took a geography test today and I'm praying to God." Well, her mom thought it was pretty cool that Suzy trusted God enough to pray about her schoolwork—until Suzy went on to say, "I'm praying for God to please make London the capital of France."

There are some obvious reasons why God does not make London the capital of France. But what about other prayers? Prayers of desperation. Prayers for restored health, a dying child, a broken marriage—perfectly reasonable and urgent prayers about heartbreaking circumstances.

A good and loving God would grant those kinds of requests, right? So why doesn't he? The pain of unanswered prayer can gnaw at us like a growling stomach reminds us of an unmet need. The enemy would like us to believe that God does not heed our requests because he is apathetic or insufficient. Or perhaps, Satan whispers, the problem lies with us. Maybe we are the ones who are insufficient in faith, goodness, or methodology. To add to our frustration, we may find the words of Jesus confusing when he says,

I say to you, ask, and it will be given you; search, and you will find; knock, and the door will be opened for you. For everyone who asks receives, and everyone who searches finds, and for everyone who knocks, the door will be opened. Is there anyone among you who, if your child asks for a fish, will give a snake instead of a fish? Or if the child asks for an egg, will give a scorpion? If you then, who are evil, know how to give good gifts to your children, how much more will the heavenly Father give the Holy Spirit to those who ask him! (Luke 11:9–13).

These words may seem to be a blanket promise with no conditions. If I ask for a lifetime's supply of caramel, is God obligated to give it to me? Obviously not. God is not a cosmic genie who serves my every whim and while on the surface, all that caramel may seem like a good gift, it probably has a downside.

I believe God is saying that whatever we ask according to his will, will be granted. How do we know what is his will? By knowing him. The closer we get to God, the more attuned we are to what he desires for us, and what he desires for us is to give us good gifts. If you are a parent, you totally get this. You delight in giving your children good things. But really, if you love anyone, and they were in need, wouldn't you want to give them what they needed if you could? So if we, who love imperfectly and sporadically, want to give to others, how much more will God, who loves perfectly and unconditionally, want to give to us? And what he desires to give to us, the scripture says, is the Holy Spirit. What better gift can there be?

If we understood the gifts God has for us, perhaps we would be much more apt to ask. Remember, God is a giver. Paul reminds us: "He who did not withhold his own Son, but gave him up for all of us, will he not with him also give us everything else?" (Rom. 8:32).

The purpose of prayer is prayer. In other words, God's desire is for us to be in a relationship with him. That relationship is the most important one of our lives. Prayer is not about a set of principles; it is about a person. It is not about following all the rules so we can obtain our laundry list of requests. It is about spending time with a God who wants to spend time with us.

Like any relationship, our relationship with God needs to be tended. Also, as in any relationship, there are obstacles in communication. Let us explore three possible hindrances to effective prayers.

Unbelief: If we have a hard time believing God can do what God says he can do, then our prayers are weighed down with clouds of doubt. If we do not believe God, it stands to reason we do not trust God. We are like the woman whose horse-drawn carriage ran away. When the hero rescued the woman, she said, "I trusted God until he took away the reins."[30] In reality, she did not trust God at all. She trusted the reins, and when they broke, she blamed God. She trusted God as long as she was in control, but when she realized she was not in control, the story changed.

One day Jesus is telling his friends that if they have enough faith in God, they can move mountains into the sea. Unbelief, according to Jesus, is the only thing that stands in the way of making this a reality. He goes on to say, "So I tell you, whatever you ask for in prayer, believe that you have received it, and it will be yours" (Mark 11:24). Ask and believe.

One time, a father brought his son to Jesus because the boy was possessed. The father pleads, "If you are able to do anything, have pity on us and help us." Jesus says to him, "If you are able! All things can be done for the one who believes." Immediately the father cries out, "I believe; help my unbelief!" (Mark 9:23–24).

Jesus is our example for prayer. He said to God in the garden of Gethsemane, before his arrest and death, "Abba, Father, for you all things are possible; yet, not what I want, but what you want" (Mark 14:36). He believed God could do anything he asked, but he also was close enough to his Father to know that God's plan was what was best. The kind of prayer that moves mountains is prayer for the fruitfulness of God's kingdom.

Unforgiveness: Jesus is clear: "Forgive us our sins, for we ourselves forgive everyone indebted to us" (Luke 11:4). Often, we respond to that imperative with, "Yes, but. . . .": "Yes, but nothing I did is as bad as what they did to me;" "Yes, but you have no idea how hurt I am;" "Yes, but they were really out of line."

To which God says, "Yes, but how can you ever look down on another person or hold a grudge after an honest evaluation of your own heart?" The Lord makes it clear: let go of self-righteous unforgiveness and heal your broken relationships, as far as it is up to you. Paul says, "Make every effort to live in peace with everyone" (Heb. 12:14 NIV). God wants us to carry his relationship with us into our relationship with others.

Unconfessed sin: You cannot have an honest relationship if you are not honest. It is that simple. Isaiah says our sins have separated us from God and if those sins are not acknowledged, God will not hear us (Isa. 59:2). King David committed adultery and murder. He painfully recognized that when he kept silent about the wrong he had done, he wasted away; however, when he admitted his wrongdoing, he was forgiven and his relationship with God was restored (Ps. 51).

Consider these three things: unbelief, unforgiveness, and unconfessed sin.

I could stop here, and just tell you to believe, forgive, and confess, and your prayer life will be amazing. But that leaves me a bit worried—and feeling inadequate. Does that mean that God only answers the prayers of those who have all their ducks in a row? I know each of these facets are important, but I am a broken person living in a broken world. And if it is left up to me, surely, I will fail.

And what about those times when I have felt close to God, my relationships were intact, I had confessed all my sins, and it still felt as if God wasn't hearing me? What the heck?

Perhaps we are asking the wrong questions. Perhaps the question is not why some prayers are answered and some are not. The real question is, why does God answer any prayer at all?

Jesus tells a parable about a tax collector and a Pharisee, a religious leader of the day, who go to the temple to pray. The Pharisee brags about how good he is, and the tax collector simply says, "God, be merciful to me, a sinner!" Jesus says it is the tax collector who goes away forgiven (Luke 18:9–14). This story proves that God hears the prayers of the inadequate. Thank goodness— because if he did not, he would not hear mine.

What is God's motivation for answering any of us? If there is no correlation between our goodness and God's positive response to our prayers, why do we even bother? Why does *God* even bother?

Perhaps it will make more sense if we know what God is like before we question why he does what he does.

Christian author, radio broadcaster, and former seminary professor Steve Brown, in his book *Approaching God: Accepting the Invitation to Stand in the Presence of God*, explains it this way: Suppose you see a man with a knife going toward a person who is strapped down on a table and helpless. You might think this knife-wielding man is a monster about to commit an unthinkable crime. But would you still think that if I told you that the man with a knife is a surgeon and the helpless victim strapped down on a table is the patient?[31] It takes on a whole different meaning, right?

It is desperately important that we know what God is like before we question what he does or does not do. If God is a monster, our unanswered prayers mean something quite different from those prayers to a loving, grace-filled Father. The Bible teaches that God is not only loving, but that he is the only one who is in charge. His ways and thoughts are beyond our range (Isa. 55:8–9).

This leaves us with a choice. We can look at unanswered prayer and wonder if God is a puppeteer who delights in toying with our circumstances; or we can look at unanswered prayers and say, "Papa, I just don't understand, but I trust you."

When my oldest son was eleven, he fell off his bike and broke his leg. His femur twisted apart, and the doctor had to pull his bone back into its proper position so they could set the leg. I will never forget how difficult it was to stand beside my son's hospital bed as they attached weights to his broken leg. I stood over him, cupped his cheeks in my hands, looked him in the eye, and tried to distract him from the incredible pain he was about to experience. As I held his face in my hands, I tried to make him lock his eyes on me, but he was too distracted by what the doctor was doing and he kept screaming, "No, mommy, don't let them do it. I'm just a little boy. I'm just a little boy."

It was one of the hardest situations I have ever been in, but it had to be done. My son did not understand it. It hurt like crazy. He cried, I cried, but the motivation was never to cause needless pain. It was not an act of malice or incompetence. Was I an uncaring mother for letting the doctor inflict such pain on my little boy? Or was it an act of love and healing?

The next time your prayers are not answered in the way you would like them to be answered, ask yourself these two questions: 1) Does God love me? 2) Do I trust him?

The proper answers to these questions—the truth— will not make your pain go away but they will remind you God is there, he loves you, he knows what he is doing, and that, even if you do not understand why, he does.

It has been said that God always answers prayers: sometimes "yes," sometimes "no," and sometimes "not yet." Even the disciples struggled with prayer, asking Jesus to "Teach us to pray" (Luke 11:1). Prayer is hard, and Satan would have you believe God does not love you and that you cannot trust him—so why bother? Baptist preacher Charles Spurgeon reminds us of the truth: "If you can't trace God's hand, trust his heart."

For Personal or Group Study:

Thoughts to Consider

- What has been your experience with unanswered prayer?
- Have you ever felt as though God was not listening to you?
- Do you assume God does not answer your prayers because you are not worthy?
- Do you believe God can grant what you request?

- Is there unconfessed sin in your life?
- Is there someone you are having a hard time forgiving? (If so, see chapter 14.)
- Why does God answer any prayer at all?

Detect the Lie

- God only answers the prayers of the faithful.
- Unanswered prayer is God's way of testing me.
- God toys with humanity like a cruel puppeteer.
- It is foolish to put my hope and trust in such a distant God.
- If I had more faith, God would answer my prayers.
- Some people have a better "pipeline" to God than others.

Argue against the Lie

- God always has my best interests in mind. He is good all the time; and all the time, he is good.
- If I ask for anything that is within God's will, he will grant it to me.
- Sometimes we do not have because we do not ask.
- Prayer is powerful and effective.
- Just because God seems silent does not mean he is not there.
- I may never understand or get an answer to the "why" questions of life.
- Persistence in prayer is effective.

Replace the Lie with the Truth (God's Word)

- "And he said to them, 'Suppose one of you has a friend, and you go to him at midnight and say to him, "Friend, lend me three loaves of bread; for a friend of mine has arrived, and I have nothing to set before him." And he answers from within, "Do not bother me; the door has already been locked, and my children are with me in bed; I cannot get up and give you anything." I tell you, even though he will not get up and give him anything because he is his friend, at least because of his persistence he will get up and give him whatever he needs. So I say to you, Ask, and it will be given you; search, and you will find; knock, and the door will be opened for you. For everyone who asks receives, and everyone who searches finds, and for everyone who knocks, the door will be opened. Is there anyone among you who, if your child asks for a fish, will give a snake instead of a fish? Or if the child asks for an egg, will give a scorpion? If you then, who are evil, know how to give good gifts to your children, how much more will the heavenly Father give the Holy Spirit to those who ask him!'" (Luke 11:5–13).

- "And this is the boldness we have in him, that if we ask anything according to his will, he hears us. And if we know that he hears us in whatever we ask, we know that we have obtained the requests made of him" (1 John 5:14–15).

- "So I tell you, whatever you ask for in prayer, believe that you have received it, and it will be yours" (Mark 11:24).

- "Rejoice in hope, be patient in suffering, persevere in prayer" (Rom. 12:12).

- "You do not have, because you do not ask. You ask and do not receive, because you ask wrongly, in order to spend what you get on your pleasures" (James 4:2–3).

- "Make this your common practice: Confess your sins to each other and pray for each other so that you can live together whole and healed. The prayer of a person living right with God is something powerful to be reckoned with" (James 5:16 MSG).

CHAPTER 14

STUCK IN the mud of self-pity

*"[Job said,] 'I loathe my life; I will give free utterance
to my complaint; I will speak in the bitterness
of my soul'"*

(Job 10:1).

The online Urban Dictionary defines self-pity as "especially exaggerated or self-indulgent pity where you believe that you are the victim who has done no wrong and is deserving of condolence from everyone." It is also described this way: "Self-pity is easily the most destructive of the non-pharmaceutical narcotics; it is addictive, gives momentary pleasure and separates the victim from reality."[32]

Sounds about right. Who has not had an occasional "woe is me" moment? When self-pity washes over me, I give myself a time limit. I allow myself to wallow for an hour or so, but then I know I must pull myself together and move on. Sometimes it works—sometimes not so much.

Feeling sorry for yourself is usually the result of 1) I did not get what I wanted, or 2) I got what I did not want. These feelings are two sides of the same coin: "I deserve this," or "I don't deserve this"—which is another way of saying we are plagued with entitlement and pride.

Self-pity becomes dangerous when we cannot get past it. Satan would love to have us wallowing in self-pity, absorbed in our own pain, and feeling like a victim. We cannot live an abundant life when we are stuck in the mud.

When I was going through my divorce, I had many instances of wallowing in self-pity. Now divorce was a part of my identity. I believed I would forever be labeled as someone who could not keep a husband. My children would not be raised in a nuclear family. It sucked. Big time.

As tempting as it was to blame my ex-husband and stay the victim, I knew that was exactly where the enemy wanted me. I had to move past my anger, or the rage was going to kill me. Maybe not literally, but spiritually and emotionally. Forgiveness seemed to be the only way to pull myself out of the self-pity pit.

Before the divorce, I slowly felt my marriage slipping away. There were many signs and red flags. One weekend when my husband was out of town, I was cleaning our house and found the proof I dreaded, but I was not totally surprised. It became undisputable that my husband was having an affair.

Before I go any further, I want to point out that while my husband had an affair, the demise of our marriage was on both of us. It is always a two-way street, and I am not blameless in this story.

Also let me say that my "wasband" (a term I like better than "ex") is a wonderful dad and an amazing partner in raising our boys. We were able to reach the point where we worked well together for the sake of our sons, and I was able to work through what I needed to work through to forgive him. But the "other woman" was a different story.

At the mention of her name, my stomach knotted, and my mind filled with red. I fantasized running her over with my car. It is correct to say I hated her, and forgiveness seemed too far out of reach.

Seven years after our divorce, I was in a fabric store picking out material for curtains and soon realized that she too was in the store. My stomach churned and I felt sick. My wasband informed me earlier that week that the two of them were moving in together. I knew what that meant, and it made my heart sink. It meant she would be a part of my children's lives, so I knew I had to figure out how to forgive her or be torn apart every time I saw her. She came up to me in the fabric store and before I knew it, I was agreeing to have lunch with her. Later that week, we met and my journey to forgive her began.

I learned much on that journey and pray that my experience may help you if you have someone in your life you need to forgive. While you may not have been hurt in the same way I was, the hope is you can find the strength to forgive and be healed so that you are no longer stuck in the self-pity pit. Here are some things to remember, and to do, as you learn to forgive.

Forgiveness is a process. In the Lord's Prayer, we ask God to forgive us as we forgive those who have sinned against us (Matt. 6:12). I felt hypocritical asking God to forgive me when I could not forgive her. I began to realize that I could not forgive on my own. I needed God's help. So, my prayer became, "Forgive me my sins, and help me forgive those who have sinned against me." We are to pray for those who persecute us (a.k.a. our enemies). She felt like an enemy to me. Her presence persecuted me. But I included her and my wasband in my prayers every night. Sometimes all I was able to muster was a mention of their names (and tried not to do it with a sneer).

Acknowledge the hurt and know that it is OK to be angry with God. Every now and then, the emotions still come flooding back. Something triggers the humiliation and anger of the affair, and I am right back to the moment I discovered it. In my journaling and in my prayers of those days, I shook my fist at God. What did I do to deserve this pain? Why me?

I believe God would much rather we come to him with our hurt and anger than suppress it or express it to everyone else but him, or let it come out sideways and lash out at others (kick-the-dog syndrome). The Psalms are full of King David's questioning and anger. Just as I would much rather my own child come to me when angry or hurt, God wants us to yell at him and pound our fists on his chest. Did I deserve what happened to me? No. Do you deserve what happened to you? No. Do we understand it? Probably not. And the offense hurts. And we are angry.

Remember, anger is a human emotion or feeling created by God and it is found throughout the Bible (see chapter 18). The tragedy is in using our anger as an excuse to sin. Many times, especially when I went out with friends, I bad-mouthed this woman. I wanted everyone else to hate her as much as I did, and I wanted to be sure they all knew what she had done. But my hurt did not give me the right to sin. I tried to hold my tongue. Sometimes I succeeded; most times I did not. Then it was my asking for forgiveness from God.

Forgiveness is not the same as tolerance. Author Lewis B. Smedes says, "You can forgive almost anything. But you cannot tolerate everything. . . . We don't have to tolerate what people do just because we forgive them for doing it. Forgiving heals us personally. To tolerate everything only hurts us all in the long run."[33]

Forgiving does not make you a doormat or mean you condone a behavior. I do not believe it means we are to forget what the other person has done. You can learn from the experience. You do not have to have a relationship with that person. Smedes says, "Forgiveness is God's invention for coming to terms with a world in which people are unfair to each other and hurt each other deeply. He began by forgiving us. And he invites us all to forgive each other."[34]

Slay the monster. I needed to kill the monster my imagination created her to be. I hated her so badly; I could not stand the mention of her name. But God ended up bringing us together in that fabric store. The day I found out about the affair, I called her on the phone and asked, "How long have you been sleeping with my husband?" Note to self: probably not smart to make such phone calls until one has settled down. But there we were, face to face, making a lunch date.

Slowly, she began to join the human race for me again. She was not the embodiment of evil I had created her to be. She was a flawed, fallible human being—not much different from me. I had to rediscover the humanity of the person who had wronged me, just as God treated my wrongs by showing me mercy and grace. I have never had an affair but there are no degrees of sin. All sin separates us from God, and all of us have fallen short (Rom. 3:23), but the atoning work of Christ covers all of it. It is a slap in the face of Jesus to say that my sins are such that they should be forgiven but hers are not. When God asks us to forgive, he is asking us to see him in the other person, to open ourselves up to the other person's humanness—and to our own.

Give up the right to get even. Every moral instinct tells us we have the right to balance the scales. But the Bible tells us that vengeance belongs, by right, only to God (Rom. 12:19). God will balance the scales, as he is the only one who understands the entirety of the situation. Only he knows the condition of the heart.

In a way, I felt hatred was my revenge, but my hatred was not hurting anyone but me. My self-pity and anger were hurting only me. The person we are trying to forgive may not even know—or care—that we are angry. As novelist Anne Lamott suggests, "Not forgiving is like drinking rat poison and then waiting for the rat to die." Since revenge is not the answer, God gave us forgiveness.

How can we live in a world where people hurt each other? God said he tried forgiveness and it worked for him. He invites us—*commands* us—to try the same on each other. Forgiveness is God's answer to living in a hurtful world.

Remove yourself from the center of the offense. I remember being so dumbfounded. How could they do this to me? What were they thinking every time they were together? Did they hate me that much? How could they do this to my (our!) children?

A wise counselor set me straight. The truth of the matter was that they were not thinking of me at all. They were only thinking of themselves.

Sometimes we do not have the luxury of repentance. I was fortunate. I was able to face the people I blamed for all my pain, and they said they were sorry. That is not always the case. Often the person who hurts us may not even be aware of the pain they caused or, even worse, not care. So, you wonder, does that person deserve to be forgiven? The short answer is no. *No one* deserves to be forgiven. Forgiveness is not something we earn but is an act of grace that reaches down into our humanity, recognizes our failure, and sets us squarely in the grace of God.

People will let you down. If you are looking to people to determine your happiness or satisfaction, you will be disappointed. Sometimes we can forgive people for what they do—but it can be hard to forgive them for who they are. Look deep into your resentments of other people. Do you resent them for what they have done—or because of who they are? Do you resent them because they have not fulfilled some expectation or standard you have put on them? Have they failed to meet your needs?

God forgives us for what we do. He does not forgive us for who we are. He accepts us for who we are—flawed, fallible human beings.

Eventually—two steps forward, one step back—I came to forgive this woman. That is my story, but it may not be your story. What if forgiveness seems impossible?

Jesuit priest James Martin examines how Christ asked his Father to forgive the ones who were crucifying him as he hung on the cross:

> Now, here's the big question: How do you do it? You may want to forgive but feel incapable of doing so. You want to let go of resentment, but you may honestly feel that you don't have that power within you. Well, that *wanting* to forgive is a good start, because true forgiveness is a gift from God. It's a grace. Moreover . . . even if you don't have the desire to forgive, if you have the *desire for the desire*, that's enough. God can work with that. So you may think, "Well, I can't do it," And you're right. You can't. But God can.[35]

I knew I had forgiven this woman when I began to see her as a child of God and not a source of my pain. Does that make what happened to me and my family OK? No. Can I make her and my wasband pay for the hurt they caused me? I don't want to, but even if I did want to, there is no way I can. I must keep in mind how Christ made me pay for my sins—by not making me pay at all. My debt was paid through Jesus's death and resurrection. How can I demand more than God?

Forgiveness is freeing. It is liberating to throw off that old heavy coat of bitterness and hate; it is empowering to crawl out of the pit of self-pity. When you reach that point of forgiveness, you set a prisoner free—and you soon discover that prisoner was you. Forgiveness is an experience of grace and of courage—of letting go and of moving on. It is not easy, but it is worth the effort to reach a point where the hurt finally has no power over you.

If you have been betrayed, I am sorry. If you are angry, I am sorry. If you are the one who is the offender and needs to be forgiven, say you are sorry to the one(s) you hurt if possible—and to God.

Satan would love to have you believe you are a victim. Do not let your pain define your life. If something you have done or something that has been done to you has you stuck, forgive yourself and/or them. Embrace the fact that you are flawed and fallible—just as everyone else. But you are also forgiven and free. "Lord, forgive me and help me forgive those who have sinned against me."

For Personal or Group Study:

Thoughts to Consider

- Have you ever found yourself in the pit of self-pity? How did you get out of it?

- Have you ever been angry with God? If so, does being angry with God make you feel guilty?

- Has your hurt caused you to sin? How?

- How easy is it to give up the right to get even?

- Is it necessary to hear, "I'm sorry" before you can forgive?

- Who do you need to forgive?

- Do you need to forgive yourself?

Detect the Lie

- What was done to me was too terrible to forgive.
- Forgiving someone lets them off the hook.
- If I forgive someone, I am allowing myself to become a doormat.
- I have the right to get even.
- I tried to forgive, but it didn't work.
- God should never have allowed this offense to happen to me.
- I deserve to wallow in self-pity.

Argue against the Lie

- No offense falls outside of God's grace.
- No offense is unique to you.
- We are all flawed and fallible people.
- God forgives you if you forgive others.
- Forgiveness frees you from being a victim.
- Revenge hurts no one but you.
- Self-pity is a self-destructive emotion.

Replace the Lie with the Truth (God's Word)

- "Bear with one another and, if anyone has a complaint against another, forgive each other; just as the Lord has forgiven you, so you also must forgive" (Col. 3:13).
- "For if you forgive others their trespasses, your heavenly Father will also forgive you; but if you do not forgive

others, neither will your Father forgive your trespasses" (Matt. 6:14–15).

- "Be alert. If you see your friend going wrong, correct him. If he responds, forgive him. Even if it's personal against you and repeated seven times through the day, and seven times he says, "'I'm sorry, I won't do it again,' forgive him" (Luke 17:3–4 MSG).

- "Put away from you all bitterness and wrath and anger and wrangling and slander, together with all malice, and be kind to one another, tenderhearted, forgiving one another, as God in Christ has forgiven you" (Eph. 4:31–32).

- "If we confess our sins, he who is faithful and just will forgive us our sins and cleanse us from all unrighteousness" (1 John 1:9).

- "I, even I, am he who blots out your transgressions, for my own sake, and remembers your sins no more" (Isa. 43:25 NIV).

- "As far as the east is from the west, so far he removes our transgressions from us" (Ps. 103:12).

PART 3

The Lie of Who You Are

CHAPTER 15

"For the Lord does not see as mortals see; they look on the outward appearance, but the Lord looks on the heart"

(1 Sam. 16:7).

Two little girls are looking at a scale. One says to the other, "Don't step on it; it makes you cry." How often have we equated our physical appearance with our worthiness? How often have we been defined by our body shape, height, hair color, or outward physical attributes? Our image-centric culture perpetuates an obsession with our looks.

Here is a little exercise: Make a list of what you like most about your appearance. (Go ahead, we will wait.) Now, make a list of what you like least about your appearance. Which list was easier to do? Which list was longer?

Cosmetic and clothing companies have made billions of dollars from our desire to look good. Being considered acceptable by the world is overly dependent on our outward appearance, and the images held up for us to emulate are often warped.

The cosmetic company Dove did an experiment called "Real Beauty Sketches." They asked women to describe themselves to an FBI-trained forensic artist named Gil Zamora. Zamora drew a portrait of the women based on their description. She never saw the women as she was hidden behind a curtain. Then a random stranger was asked to describe the same women to Zamora to see how the separate descriptions matched up.

The results were amazing. Two completely different portraits emerged. The second portrait was not only a more accurate rendition of the woman; it was also a more beautiful one. Below are some of the results.

To date, more than 180 million people have viewed the Real Beauty Sketches as Dove is committed to inspiring every single

KELA
as described by
KELA

KELA
as described by
A RANDOM STRANGER

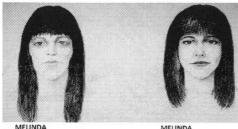

MELINDA
as described by
MELINDA

MELINDA
as described by
A RANDOM STRANGER

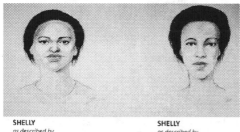

SHELLY
as described by
SHELLY

SHELLY
as described by
A RANDOM STRANGER

one of the 80 percent of women who feel anxious about how they look. They want women to remember: you are more beautiful than you think. Zamora states, "What has stayed with me are the emotional reactions the women had when they viewed the composite sketches hung side by side. I think many of these brave women realized that they had a distorted self-perception that had affected parts of their lives in significant ways."[36]

We often see ourselves differently from how we are perceived by others. It can be like looking into a funhouse mirror—our beauty is warped and distorted by the false image of what is beautiful. We are bombarded with unattainable standards of what beauty is.

Dove also has a video called "The Evolution of Beauty"[37] to demonstrate the photo-editing process involved in transforming a woman into an image good enough for mass consumption.

A relatively plain-looking model is literally transformed into a billboard-worthy supermodel. Her neck is lengthened, her eyes widened, her eyebrows arched. The before and after images are amazing.

One cosmetic commercial tagline used to be, "Maybe she's born with it. Maybe it's Maybelline." Now we know. It is more accurate to say, "Maybe it's Photoshop."

Something struck me the other day as I was lamenting over the weight I gained after my newfound love of craft beers. This thought crossed my mind: I wish I were as fat now as I thought I was at age thirty. I grew up thinking I was fat (when I was a size 8!). I also wish I had all the energy and mind-space back that I wasted obsessing over my appearance or coveting another person's appearance.

My maiden name was Lattin and large noses run in my family. I remember my Aunt Sadie had the largest nose I had ever seen on a human being. My dad's nose was also on the larger side, so it became an identifying factor for the Lattins. Growing up, I often heard the phrase, "Well, you can tell she's a Lattin by her nose." My sister and I were jealous of our sister Cindy because she inherited a nice, petite ski-slope kind of nose. We compared our noses to Cindy's nose and were left feeling self-conscious and somehow inadequate.

Here's an idea: let's put the make-up counters and cosmetic plastic surgery places out of business by refusing to compare how we look with each other and be content with our God-given attributes. Wouldn't that be something? (Just the thought of no Mary Kay makes me cringe a little. How else would I hide the cavernous pores on my big nose!?)

Much of our dissatisfaction with our looks comes from comparing ourselves with others. President Theodore Roosevelt rightly said, "Comparison is the thief of joy."

Comparisons do not stop at our appearance. We compare our parenting, our possessions, our accomplishments, our relationships—and the list goes on and on.

I will be honest with you—I am a star player in the game of comparison. It is not intentional. It just happens. It stems from my insecurity, competitiveness, and/or desire for perfection. I do not think my mom coined this advice, but she repeated it to me often: "There will always be someone better off than you and someone worse off than you, so quit comparing yourself to others." Thanks, Mom. You were right—again.

Comparing ourselves to others results in one of two feelings: envy or pride. We say to ourselves, "Thank goodness I am not like (or don't look like) that," which is pride. Or "I wish I had (or looked like) that," which is envy. You cannot simultaneously be happy and envious. It is one or the other.

When it comes to measuring our self-worth, God has a whole different yard stick than we do.

In the Old Testament, King Saul was on the throne when God instructed the prophet Samuel to appoint a new king. God told Samuel he would find the new king in Bethlehem and he would be the son of a man named Jesse. Jesse paraded son after handsome son in front of Samuel, but he rejected them all. God had warned Samuel against judging a person on appearance alone, saying, "Looks are not everything. Do not be impressed with his looks and stature. I have already eliminated him. God judges persons differently than humans do. Men and women look at the face; God looks into the heart" (1 Sam. 16:7 MSG).

In the end David, the youngest of Jesse's sons was anointed as king to replace Saul. Because what mattered most? His heart, not the size of his robe or the blueness of his eyes.

Isaiah talked about another servant of God, describing him this way: "He grew up before him like a tender shoot, and like a root out of dry ground. He had no beauty or majesty to attract us to him, nothing in his appearance that we should desire him" (Isa. 53:2 NIV).

It is understood by the historical rabbis of Judaism that this text is a description of the coming Christ. I find it comforting to know that Jesus had "nothing in his appearance that we should desire him." I would be disappointed to learn that Jesus got by on his stunning good looks or boyish grin. He sounds like an average Joe, and I can relate to an average Joe.

God judges a person by his or her heart, not appearance. Yet, most people spend more time maintaining and tending to their outward appearance than their inward character. I have made a promise to God that I will spend at least as much time in prayer every morning as I do in picking out my clothes for the day. Sometimes I spend a lot of time in prayer.

Another way we compare ourselves to others occurs in the parable Jesus tells of workers in a vineyard. A landowner needed workers, so he went out around 9 a.m. and hired guys hanging around the town square. He agreed to pay them the usual daily wage. The landowner went again at noon, at 3 p.m., and at 5 p.m. to hire additional laborers. When the workday ended, all the workers lined up to receive their wages. Strangely, the last ones hired were paid the same amount as the ones hired at 9 in the morning. "What!" the early workers complained. "Why do they receive the same wage as us when we bore the heat of the day?"

The landowner explained he did no wrong. He paid the workers what they agreed upon. He asks, "Am I not allowed to do what I choose with what belongs to me? Or are you envious because I'm generous?" (Matt. 20:1–16).

I love (and hate) this story because it is a hint of God's grace, yet it grates on my sense of fairness. It also shows us how prone we are to compare our circumstances with another's and lament, "That's not fair!"

Upon closer examination of my heart, I find I identify with those hired first ("firsties"). I have believed in God all my life and have worked hard for his kingdom. I was hired early in the morning. That should count for something.

But what of the "lasties"—those who showed up at the very end? They have hardly done anything to merit God's grace. Firsties judge God to be unfair because he gives lasties what they have not worked for and do not deserve.

The hard and glorious truth is: at the foot of the cross, we are all lasties. Not one of us has done anything to deserve the grace of God. So yes, God is unfair. Wondrously, gloriously, lavishly unfair. He gives us what we need, not what we deserve.

How can you tell if you are a firstie or a lastie? Jesus has given us some clues.

- Those who think of themselves as last respond to life with gratitude.
- Those who think of themselves as first respond to life with grumbling.

Are you grumbling more than you are giving thanks? It is easy to do. Do you find yourself praying, "God, it's not fair! I do (or do not) deserve this"? Grumbling springs from the notion we deserve more than we receive. Gratitude comes from realizing we receive far more than we deserve.

Here is another clue:

- Those who think of themselves as last are content.
- Those who think of themselves as first are always comparing.

You cannot simultaneously be grateful and envious. Perhaps that is why God made the commandment, "Do not covet," one of his top ten. He knew our penchant for jealousy and fairness.

God's grace and the gospel put to death any form of comparison. When it comes to the grace of God, it does not matter where you fall in line. Jesus will offend all who assume that a good spot in the line must be earned. He will offend all who think grace is a ranking system.

Even the workers hired early in the day rolled out of bed that morning unemployed. They were just as unemployed as those who were hired at the end of the day. This story is not about fairness or earned wages or reimbursement. It is an illustration of a gracious and undeserved gift offered freely by a gracious and generous God. He does not give us what we deserve; he gives us what we need—and what we need is God himself.

When it comes to our appearance, are we content or comparing? Are we grateful for our earthly temple or do we grumble? Does our appearance say anything about our worth in the eyes of our Maker?

In 2001, the movie *Shallow Hal* was released. Hal Larson is a superficial man whose fixation on the physical beauty of women gets in the way of seeing their inner beauty. After a chance meeting, he is hypnotized, and he begins to see women based on the condition of their heart, not their body. He meets Rosemary, a generous, kind woman who is used to being ignored by men due to her morbid obesity. But to Hal, who is seeing her inner beauty as her outward appearance, thinks she is the most charming, precious woman he knows and falls in love with her. He no longer judges others according to their outward appearance, but by the condition of their heart. Can we do the same?

For Personal or Group Study:

Thoughts to Consider

- What are some of the false images of beauty you see around you?

- Do you covet someone's physical attribute(s)?

- If you could change one feature about the way you look, what would it be?

- What part of your appearance do you appreciate?

- What is the danger of believing, "I am how I appear"?

- Does the story of the workers in the vineyard bother you? Why?

- Do you respond to life with grumbling or gratitude?

- For the most part, are you content or comparing?

Detect the Lie

- The standard of beauty held up by the world is real and attainable.

- My physical attributes determine my worth.

- If I could change my appearance, I would be happier.

- Not everyone deserves God's grace.

- Everyone is judging me, so I have the right to judge them.

Argue against the Lie

- No part of my appearance changes my status with God.

- No part of my appearance determines my worth.

- Even if I could change my appearance, I would find something else wrong.

- God looks at your heart, not your appearance.

- God's grace is not earned but given freely.

- Life is not fair.

- It is not your job to make life fair.

Replace the Lie with the Truth (God's Word)

- "Do not let your adorning be external—the braiding of hair and the putting on of gold jewelry, or the clothing you wear—but let your adorning be the hidden person of the heart with the imperishable beauty of a gentle and quiet spirit, which in God's sight is very precious" (1 Pet. 3:3–4 ESV).

- "Charm is deceitful, and beauty is vain, but a woman who fears the Lord is to be praised" (Prov. 31:30).

- "So you also on the outside look righteous to others, but inside you are full of hypocrisy and lawlessness" (Matt. 23:28).

- "Physical exercise has some value, but spiritual exercise is much more important, for it promises a reward in both this life and the next" (1 Tim. 4:8 GNT).

- "We do not dare to classify or compare ourselves with some who commend themselves. When they measure themselves by themselves and compare themselves with themselves, they are not wise" (2 Cor. 10:12 NIV).

- "Or do you not know that your body is a temple of the Holy Spirit within you, which you have from God, and that you are not your own? For you were bought with a price; therefore glorify God in your body" (1 Cor. 6:19–20).

- "But God told Samuel, 'Looks aren't everything. Don't be impressed with his looks and stature. I've already eliminated him. God judges persons differently than humans do. Men and women look at the face; God looks into the heart'" (1 Sam. 16:7 MSG).

- "A heart at peace gives life to the body, but envy rots the bones" (Prov. 14:30 NIV).

CHAPTER 16

*"So whether you eat or drink or whatever you do,
do it all for the glory of God"*

(1 Cor. 10:31).

In our society of doers, what we "do" is paramount to determining who we are. When meeting a new person, the conversation usually moves from exchanging names to asking, "So, what do you do?" We use the answer to that question to make conclusions about a person's intelligence, education, income, and value to society. We too find our worth in our work. Retirement or job loss is hard, because so much of our identity is gleaned from what we "do."

When I left my job as the editor-in-chief of a local parenting magazine, I struggled. For thirteen years, that was who I was, and now that was no longer true. Even though I left because I entered a new career that I was excited about, I still mourned the loss of this part of my identity.

I remember seeing the first issue of the magazine after I had left. It was difficult to crack open the cover and see what was inside. A part of me hoped it was awful. Maybe there would be misspellings and stupid stories and bad graphics. Wouldn't that say something about my worth as a person if the magazine failed miserably without my capable hands to guide it?

Yeah, right. It was beautifully done, well laid out, and I did not see one typo. Intellectually, I knew my desire to see it fail was wrong and misguided, but I could not quiet the voice deep down in my psyche that told me my worth was wrapped up in my ability to do my job better than another person's. I believed the fallacy that what I did and how well I did it determined my worth.

When it comes to allowing comparison to steal our joy, the same is true for what we accomplish. When my children were little, I straddled the world of working and being a stay-at-home mom. What I found was interesting. People who stayed at home with their little ones looked down on me because I was not completely committed to being a full-time mom. People who worked looked down on me because I was not completely committed to my professional career.

The truth is we all have purpose and meaning regardless of our occupation or vocation. What we do is not the core of our identity, but how we do the work put before us is important.

The reformer Martin Luther had much to say about the topic of vocation. In his day, the term "vocation" only applied to priests and those called by God into service for God. He recaptured this word and used it instead to refer to every calling a person might fulfill: office worker, farmer, baker, plumber, wife, father, civil servant, and so on. It is not important what we do but how we do it. We are to do work to the best of our ability, which glorifies God because we are using the gifts he gave us, and we are to do it in service to our neighbor, because "God doesn't need our good works; our neighbors do."[38]

For most of us, a large part of our life is spent at work; therefore, whether or not we like our job speaks volumes to the quality of our life. Statistically, that quality is not good. One poll shows 70 percent of Americans are not engaged in their jobs.[39] Patrick Lencioni, a business management writer, studied what factors created a satisfactory job. You would think it would be factors such as salary, working conditions, possibility of advancement, and job responsibilities. But in his book, *Three Signs of a Miserable Job,* Lencioni says such factors are not the case.

Lencioni says, "A professional basketball player can be miserable in his job while the janitor cleaning the locker room behind him finds fulfillment in his work. A marketing executive can be miserable making a quarter of a million dollars a year while the waitress who serves her lunch derives meaning and satisfaction from her job." These findings led Lencioni to research job satisfaction, and he discovered three factors people desire from their work:

1. To be known: People want to be recognized, understood, and appreciated for their efforts.

2. To be relevant: People want to know "who am I helping?" and "how am I helping?" They want their work to have purpose and impact.

3. To be measurable: People want to see a clear, observable link between their daily job responsibilities and the metric they will be measured against.[40]

It probably does not surprise you that we want to be known, relevant, and possess the ability to measure improvement. If what we do is relevant to who we are, then we want satisfaction and fulfillment from our employment. There is nothing wrong with that desire. The problem comes when we let our accomplishments become a determining factor of our worth, when God desires to be the one who fulfills the markers of satisfaction. Let's look at those same factors from God's perspective.

In Christ we are known: Jesus tells us that he, the Good Shepherd, opens the gate for us, and calls us by name. Like sheep who know their shepherd, we follow him because he knows us and we know his voice (John 10:3–4). God tells us, "Do not fear, for I have redeemed you; I have called you by name, you are mine" (Isa. 43:1). Before we were formed in the womb God knew us (Ps. 139:13). In Christ, everyone is someone, and we are known.

In Christ, we are relevant: The love Jesus has for us is not just sentimental. We, as a part of his flock, can make a difference in the world. We are not saved *from* something but saved *for* something. Jesus says, "As the Father has sent me, so I send you" (John 20:21). We are called to make a difference in the lives of others—to fulfill our vocation as best we can.

How do we measure our progress? All the things that typically mark success in the world do not add up to a hill of beans in the eyes of God. You could say the measuring stick for a job well done is Christ himself. Did we bring a little bit of light into the world today? When we messed up, did we make amends? Were our actions constructive or destructive?

Oswald Chambers says, "Our spiritual life cannot be measured by success as the world measures it, but only by what God pours through us—and we cannot measure that at all."[41]

Perhaps we are hard-wired with the propensity to measure progress and count accomplishments. I am the type of person who lives off a to-do list and finds great joy in checking off completed tasks. If I accomplish something not on my to-do list, I write it in so I can check that task off. (You too?)

When my boys were little, they played tee-ball. It was such a joy to watch them out on the diamond in their little uniforms and floppy baseball mitts. Often, when a player approached the ball balanced on the tee, he would stand on the wrong side of the batter's box and the coach would gently turn the player around and then hurriedly get out of the way before getting smacked by a swinging bat. If the young player did hit the ball, the chance he would run to first base was just as good as the chance he would run to third. Outfielders were often more interested in wrestling their buddy than scooping up a ground ball.

One day in the middle of a game, their beloved kindergarten teacher, Mrs. Pobst, was walking from the parking lot toward the field to watch the game. The minute she was spotted, the entire field cleared as they all ran to give her a hug.

The team could not have cared less what inning it was or who had the most hits. Their goal was not to win but to enjoy this time together. They were living the life, enjoying their friends, hugging the teacher. It is adults who make everything about who is winning. We turn everything into a competition and fret over the score.

God is not like that. He does not care if we ran to third base instead of first or let the ball dribble past our glove. He knows we are going to take our eye off the ball now and then. It is OK. He is just thrilled we are in the game.

And while we are in the game, we do have one task. The only "job" Jesus had was to accomplish the will of his Father. We are invited to do the same, and when we do, we fulfill our truest purpose. Scripture tells us:

> "Everyone who is called by my name, whom I created for my glory, whom I formed and made" (Isa. 43:7).

> "Use your whole body as an instrument to do what is right for the glory of God" (Rom. 6:13 NLT).

> "Everything comes from God alone. Everything lives by his power, and everything is for his glory" (Rom. 11:36 TLB).

"So whether you eat or drink or whatever you do, do it all for the glory of God" (1 Cor 10:31).

Are you noticing a trend? Our job is to glorify God. That is it. It was Christ's purpose too. In the garden of Gethsemane, he prays, "Father, the hour has come; glorify your Son so that the Son may glorify you. . . . I have brought you glory on earth by finishing the work you gave me to do. And now, Father, glorify me in your presence with the glory I had with you before the world began" (John 17:1, 4–5 NIV).

But here is the kicker about glorifying God: he does not need us to give him glory; he already has it. C. S. Lewis said, "A man can no more diminish God's glory by refusing to worship Him than a lunatic can put out the sun by scribbling the word 'darkness' on the walls of his cell."[42]

God did not create us because he needed someone to love and adore him. He already had that with his Son and the Spirit. God already had love and adoration far purer and more powerful than anything we could give him. God did not create us to receive joy; he created us to give joy—to him and to each other. He created us so we too could experience the love, joy, and peace we were created to have. When we glorify our Maker, he, in turn, glorifies us.

When I was younger, I was always asking God, "What is my purpose?" I was desperately trying to figure out what God wanted me to do. I wanted my work to be meaningful and my purpose clear. I wanted to make a difference for the kingdom of God. That is fine and dandy, but it means nothing if I put what I do for God ahead of having a relationship with God. I do not want to work for God; I want to work *with* God. Working for God can be exhausting because then it is up to me, whereas working with God is exhilarating. Every day is an adventure, and I can leave the heavy lifting to him.

We are invited to seek first the kingdom of God. Job #1 is to tend to our relationship with God. Then we become aligned with our purpose because it is through our relationship with God—not our hard work, good theology, or stunning people skills—that God will be glorified. "But seek first his kingdom and his righteousness, and all these things will be given to you as well." (Matt. 6:33 NIV).

Accomplishments and careers are not wrong, but in the end our identity is so much richer than what we do for eight hours a day or the number of check marks on our to-do list. Whether we are picking up garbage or sitting in a cubicle, our identity is found in Christ.

For Personal or Group Study:

Thoughts to Consider

- How does what you "do" define you?
- Do any of your accomplishments cause God to love you more?
- Do any of your failures cause God to love you less?
- What is the danger of believing, "I am what I accomplish"?
- How do you define glorifying God?
- Do you struggle to find purpose in your life?
- How important is it for you to feel known? Relevant?
- How do you measure success?

Detect the Lie

- The busier I am, the more purpose my life has.
- I must be successful and productive to have value.
- My job (and/or paycheck) determines my worth.
- If I take time to relax, rewind, or spend time in quietness, I am being lazy.
- There is no way I can glorify God in my current job.
- I have to do all the work or nothing will get done.

Argue against the Lie

- None of my accomplishments, or lack of accomplishments, change my status with God.
- No part of my job determines my worth.
- My paycheck is not a reflection of my value as a person.
- I am saved by grace, not by works.
- Jesus needed time to rest; God even rested on the seventh day. I, too, need rest.
- You are not your job title.
- Doing your job to the best of your ability glorifies God.

Replace the Lie with the Truth (God's Word)

- "It's God's gift from start to finish! We don't play the major role. If we did, we'd probably go around bragging that we'd done the whole thing! No, we neither make nor save ourselves. God does both the making and saving" (Eph. 2:8 MSG).

- "For we are what he has made us, created in Christ Jesus for good works, which God prepared beforehand to be our way of life" (Eph. 2:10).

- "Not what you do for God but what God does for you—that's the agenda for rejoicing" (Luke 10:20 MSG).

- "Be still, and know that I am God! I am exalted among the nations, I am exalted in the earth" (Ps. 46:10).

- "He saved us, not because of any works of righteousness that we had done, but according to his mercy, through the water of rebirth and renewal by the Holy Spirit" (Titus 3:5).

- "Commit your work to the Lord, and your plans will be established" (Prov. 16:3).

- "People who don't know God and the way he works fuss over these things, but you know both God and how he works. Steep your life in God-reality, God-initiative, God-provisions. Don't worry about missing out. You'll find all your everyday human concerns will be met" (Matt. 6:33 MSG).

- "Then, because so many people were coming and going that they did not even have a chance to eat, he said to them, 'Come with me by yourselves to a quiet place and get some rest'" (Mark 6:31 NIV).

- "Whatever your hand finds to do, do with your might" (Eccl. 9:10).

- "For from him and through him and to him are all things. To him be the glory forever. Amen" (Rom. 11:36).

CHAPTER 17

"For all that is in the world—the desire of the flesh, the desire of the eyes, the pride in riches—comes not from the Father but from the world"

(1 John 2:16).

Christian writer and speaker Tony Campolo tells a story about his youth. In his book *Who Switched the Price Tags?* he writes:

When I was a boy in Philadelphia, October 30 had special significance. The night before Halloween was designated as Mischief Night. On that night, the adults of our neighborhood braced themselves against all sorts of petty "crimes" at the hands of the younger generation. Windows were soaped, air was let out of tires—all the annoying mischief an adolescent mind could conjure up we did. One year, my best friend and I devised what we thought was a brilliant and creative plan for mischief. We decided to break into the basements of the local five-and-dime store. We did not plan to rob the place (Sunday School boys would never do that sort of thing); Instead, we planned to do something that, as far as the owner of the store was concerned, would have been far worse. Our plan was to get into that five-and-dime store and change the price tags on things.

We imagined what it would be like the next morning when people came into the store and discovered that radios were selling for a quarter and bobby pins were priced at five dollars each. With diabolical glee, we wondered what it would be like in that store when nobody could figure out what the prices of things really should be.

Sometimes, I think that Satan has played the same kind of trick on all of us. Sometimes, I think he has broken into our lives and changed the price tags on things.[43]

This story paints a picture of our world today. We are a society of consumers who know the price of items but the value of nothing. Often, we look to what we acquire to define our worth and project an image of who we are.

The PBS show *Frontline* aired a documentary called *The Persuaders*. It took an in-depth look at the multibillion-dollar industries of advertising and public relations, and how, in an effort to better understand and capture the cynical consumer, these "persuasion industries" have changed the face of advertising.

It used to be that promoting products meant the advertiser emphasized what the product did. Correspondent Douglas Rushkoff said, "Ads laid claim to real, tangible differences between one product and another." They were based on what advertising expert Kevin Roberts called "er" words—whiter, brighter, cleaner, stronger. But at some point, Rushkoff explains, "these words ceased to have meaning. We no longer believed that one product was any brighter or cleaner than any other."

By the early 1990s, a new approach to advertising emerged. Naomi Klein, author of *No Logo,* says, "Consumers are like roaches. You spray them and spray them, and after a while, it doesn't work anymore." So, to win consumer loyalty, most advertisers no longer talked about what the product did, but focused on what the product meant.

This tactic is called "spiritual" or "emotional" marketing. Advertising today tries to form a spiritual or emotional bond between the product and the consumer's identity and need to be a part of something bigger than themselves. People are hungry to belong to a community, even if it is a community of car owners, coffee drinkers, or sneaker wearers. They long for something, anything, to give them a sense of value.

Rushkoff says, "that's the object of emotional branding: to fill the empty places where non-commercial institutions, like schools and churches, might once have done the job. Brands become more than just a mark of quality, they become an invitation to a longed-for lifestyle, a ready-made identity."

Roberts says, "The brands that move to that emotional level, that can create loyalty beyond reason, are going to be the brands where premium profits lie." The goal of advertising is to get the consumer to not just to like, admire, respect, or use the brand. "None of that wimpy-wompy stuff," he says. The goal is to get the consumer to love it and to buy into the image the product sells.[44]

When you and I are seduced by that kind of marketing, we are no longer buying a product or a brand; we are looking to our purchases to say something about who we are and how we live. We are looking to our purchases to give our lives meaning.

Take Coca-Cola for example. Its longest-running slogan, from 2009–2016, was "Open happiness." The message is: drink Coke; you will be happy. It was replaced with the current slogan, "Taste the Feeling." Marco de Quinto, Coke's chief marketing officer, maintains, "We are reinforcing that Coca-Cola is for everybody."[45] If you drink Coke, you become part of a global society that enjoys the simple pleasures of an ice-cold beverage icon.

Nike's slogan "Just Do It," was introduced in 1988. One reason this slogan has endured for so long is its call to transcendence.

It invites the consumer to dream big and join others who have made this catchphrase their personal mantra. Nike wearers belong to a community of brave, tenacious people.

Juicy Juice's print ad insinuates that you will be a good parent if you check the label on your children's juice box, just as you would check information on a helmet and training wheels on their bike ride. If you drink Dos Equis beer, you are part of the in-crowd, hobnobbing with "The Most Interesting Man in the World."

At the end of the day, it is just a can of soda, a pair of shoes, a box of juice, and a can of beer. But in our emptiness to define ourselves by what we acquire, we let our possessions define at least a part of us.

Another tactic employed by advertising agents is called "entitlement marketing." The premise is that we deserve to own the best because we work hard for it. The hair coloring product, Preference, by L'Oréal, picked up on this strategy with its tagline: "Because I'm worth it." L'Oréal was one of the most expensive hair coloring products on the shelf, but the company was reluctant to lower its price. L'Oréal turned the challenge into an opportunity to make a statement about the worth of the woman who bought it. Genius!

Burger King promotes self-admiration on its food wrappers. One wrapper proclaims: "You're special, and you deserve a special sandwich." Burger King wants you to know that you deserve to "have it your way."

The most devastating consequence of entitlement marketing is found in the promises of credit card companies. We cannot deny the consumer's culpability in irresponsible spending, but credit card mailings that promise low rates, rebates, and rewards coupled with the mentality of "I deserve this," has disastrous results.

Dr. Robert Manning, author of the book *Credit Card Nation: The Consequences of America's Addiction to Credit,* says credit is no longer viewed as an earned privilege. "This generation has been socialized [to feel] that it's an entitlement to have these kinds of lifestyles. They do not have to earn it. They do not have to be disciplined to save. As a result, credit cards have become a kind of 'yuppie food stamps.' That is a real serious impediment in terms of trying to inculcate basic financial literacy skills on this generation where they see all these abundant things in society that they think they deserve."[46]

Many other factors such as student loans and financial emergencies contribute to rising debt, but we cannot deny that advertisers have us where they want us when our purchases define who we are or are a right we deserve. America's consumer debt was approaching $14 trillion in 2019.[47] One historian describes it as "a river of red ink."

We probably know, on the intellectual level, what we acquire does not bring ultimate fulfillment. We know we cannot take our possessions with us. But we may still silently agree with rock star David Lee Roth, who once suggested, "Money can't buy you happiness, but it can buy you a yacht big enough to pull up right alongside it."

The apostle Paul writes in his letter to his mentee Timothy, "the love of money is a root to all kinds of evil" (1 Tim. 6:10). Notice it is not money that is evil, but the love of it. Our possessions or wealth, in and of themselves, are not the culprit. Satan plays on our insecurities to have us buy into the lie that our identity is not rooted in who God says we are, but in who our possessions say we are. Or, if we glean a sense of security from our possessions, he has us believe God's providence for us is not adequate.

The familiar words of the twenty-third Psalm remind us, "The Lord is my shepherd, I lack nothing" (Ps. 23:1 NIV). In God, we lack nothing. Jesus contrasts the abundant life he came to give us with the goal of the thief, Satan, who comes to steal, kill, and destroy (John 10:10). Jesus comes to give, not to receive. This word "abundant" in Greek means "exceedingly, very highly, beyond measure, more, superfluous, a quantity so abundant as to be considerably more than what one would expect or anticipate." Sounds like a good deal to me. Yet the enemy pits Jesus's promise of abundance with the mentality of scarcity. We are so worried about what we do not have that we spend precious time and energy acquiring what we do not need. The actor Will Smith says it well: "Too many people spend money they haven't earned, to buy things they don't want, to impress people they don't like." Amen. Global activist Lynne Twist, in *The Soul of Money*, talks about the shallow feeling of lack:

> For me, and for many of us, our first waking thought of the day is "I didn't get enough sleep." The next one is "I don't have enough time." Whether true or not, that thought of *not enough* occurs to us automatically before we even think to question or examine it. We spend most of the hours and the days of our lives hearing, explaining, complaining, or worrying about what we don't have enough of.
>
> We're not thin enough, we're not smart enough, we're not pretty enough or fit enough or educated or successful enough, or rich enough—ever. Before we even sit up in bed, before our feet touch the floor, we're

already inadequate, already behind, already losing, already lacking something. And by the time we go to bed at night, our minds are racing with a litany of what we didn't get, or didn't get done, that day. We go to sleep burdened by those thoughts and wake up to that reverie of lack.

This internal condition of scarcity, this mind-set of scarcity, lives at the very heart of our jealousies, our greed, our prejudice, and our arguments with life.[48]

Perhaps one reason scarcity haunts us is that we feel we do not deserve the abundant life Christ came to give us without some effort on our part. After all, we have been raised to be earners. We earn rewards, awards, grades, trust, paychecks. Yet, our voices, internal and external, say we are not enough. But here is the truth: you are right. We are not enough. Christ says you do not have to be enough, because he is enough. We can take our minds off our scarcity and grasp the abundant life Christ promises—if we could only believe it.

The Victorian Times, on September 19, 1990, reported on a twenty-four-year-old man named Danny Simpson who went to jail for robbing a bank in Ottawa. He stole $6,000 and was sent to jail for six years. He had used a .45 caliber Colt semi-automatic, which turned out to be an antique made by the Ross Rifle Company in Quebec City during WWI. At the time, the pistol was worth up to $100,000. Simpson could have walked into any gun shop and sold the pistol for at least twice the haul from his bank raid without breaking the law.[49]

Danny already had what he needed. We have all we need. An abundant life is not something to achieve—it is something to accept. A promise cannot be earned, bought, or bartered for in life. It is a sheer gift from God. Do not let the price tags get switched. Your value is found in him, not in what you acquire.

For Personal or Group Study:

Thoughts to Consider

- What is the danger of believing, "I am what I acquire"?
- Can you think of something you purchased because you thought it would project an image you desired?
- Have you ever purchased something because you thought you deserved it?
- Can you think of products that promise a certain identity or sense of belonging?
- What do your possessions say about who you are?
- Do you have everything you need—as far as possessions— in your life right now? If not, what is lacking?
- Would you define your material life as lacking, adequate, or abundant?
- In what ways do you live with an attitude of scarcity?
- How would your life be different if you lived with an attitude of abundance?
- In this world of switched price tags, are you confused about what has value and what does not?

Detect the Lie

- My worth is determined by what I own.

- My possessions provide security.
- Self-comfort is paramount.
- I deserve to own what I want and spend how I want. I work hard for it.
- I lack many things.
- The satisfaction I find in my possessions is fulfilling and permanent.
- I do not deserve an abundant life.
- Money is evil.

Argue against the Lie

- Nothing I own or do not own will change my status with God.
- My worth is not determined by my possessions or lack of possessions.
- No acquisition is guaranteed to give me security or success.
- I am to be a good steward of the treasure God has given me.
- When it comes to what I really need, I lack nothing in Christ.
- Money is not evil. The love of money is where problems begin.

Replace the Lie with the Truth (God's Word)

- "A devout life does bring wealth, but it's the rich simplicity of being yourself before God. Since we entered the world penniless and will leave it penniless, if we have bread on the table and shoes on our feet, that's enough" (1 Tim. 6:8 MSG).

- "But those who want to be rich fall into temptation and are trapped by many senseless and harmful desires that plunge people into ruin and destruction. For the love of money is a root of all kinds of evil, and in their eagerness to be rich some have wandered away from the faith and pierced themselves with many pains" (1 Tim. 6:9–10).

- "Practically everything that goes on in the world—wanting your own way, wanting everything for yourself, wanting to appear important—has nothing to do with the Father. It just isolates you from him. The world and all its wanting, wanting, wanting is on the way out—but whoever does what God wants is set for eternity" (1 John 2:16–17 MSG).

- "And the seed that fell in the weeds—well, these are the ones who hear, but then the seed is crowded out and nothing comes of it as they go about their lives worrying about tomorrow, making money, and having fun" (Luke 8:14 MSG).

- "Do not store up for yourselves treasures on earth, where moth and rust consume and where thieves break in and steal; but store up for yourselves treasures in heaven, where neither moth nor rust consumes and where thieves do not break in and steal. For where your treasure is, there your heart will be also" (Matt. 6:19–21).

- "For what will it profit them if they gain the whole world but forfeit their life? Or what will they give in return for their life?" (Matt. 16:26).

- "Do not neglect to do good and to share what you have, for such sacrifices are pleasing to God" (Heb. 13:16).

- "Then [Jesus] said to them, 'Watch out! Be on your guard against all kinds of greed; life does not consist in an abundance of possessions'" (Luke 12:15 NIV).

CHAPTER 18

"But the fruit of the Spirit is love, joy, peace, forbearance, kindness, goodness, faithfulness, gentleness and self-control"

(Gal. 25:22–23 NIV).

One night, I had a dream that my husband had been rude to me (and my husband is one of the nicest people I know). I cannot remember exactly what he did, but when I woke up, I was angry with him. It did not matter that it was just a dream; the anger I felt hung on me like an ill-fitting sweater all morning.

The other day, I met someone who I am sure is a perfectly wonderful person, but she reminded me of someone who had been a real thorn in my side in a former job. So even though all I knew about this woman was her name, I did not like her.

It is amazing how much of our life is controlled by our feelings. Some days I feel secure and confident and am ready to take on the world. Other days, the slightest crabby glance my way can send me into a tailspin. What the heck?

We often do not think of our feelings—emotional identity—as something that makes up who we are. Yet our emotions manifest our desire and fears and, in part, shape who we are. That fact is one reason feelings are so powerful—they speak to our identity. And the enemy would love it if we believed our feelings were facts—especially the negative ones—and allowed them to eat away at our emotional well-being.

If we are emotionally secure, we probably have a healthy degree of self-love. Our encounters with others reflect this stability and we are not easily swayed by our circumstances. If our self-love is waning, we may be easily offended by an off-handed remark or quickly jealous of another's success or possessions. We feel worthless and pitiful. The key word is "feel."

Feelings do not reflect truth, yet we allow ourselves to be twisted and turned by our emotions like a flag on a windy day. We give our feelings the power to determine who we are. And the problem with feelings is how they fluctuate. Perhaps we believe we could learn who we really are if we could just get in touch with our core feelings—you know, the ones that are, in our deepest heart, who we are. But which of our feelings are our core feelings?

In in my early thirties, I wanted a family. But I also wanted a career. You can have both but not without some compromises. Does that mean that one feeling was truer than the other? I want to be a size eight, but I also want to eat Oreo Double Stufs. I want to live in a warmer climate, but I also want to live near my family and friends. Feelings and desires contradict each other all the time. How do I decide which one is real? I want a Mustang convertible, but I want to be practical. (On second thought, that is a bad example. I really do want a Mustang convertible.)

Our feelings are a manifestation of our desires and fears. They are powerful and sometimes deceitful. Emotions, however, are necessary.

Feelings and emotions are two sides of the same coin, but emotions are what are called "lower-level responses." God gave them to us so we could survive everything from mammoths to hailstorms. Emotions control our fight-or-flight instincts and can be measured in physical reactions like faster heart rate, increased blood flow, and body language. Emotions precede feelings.

Feelings have to do with mental associations and reactions to emotions, which makes feelings subjective to personal experiences, beliefs, and memories. Dr. Sarah McKay, a neuroscientist and author shares this explanation: "Emotions play out in the theatre of the body. Feelings play out in the theatre of the mind."[50]

This comparison is good news because we cannot so much control our emotions, but we can control our feelings. I knew my feelings regarding the dream about my husband and the stranger who reminded me of someone else were wrong, and those feelings were easy to fix. Some negative feelings are deeply rooted and need plenty of "re-writing" to lose their destructive hold on us. Of course, we have positive feelings too that we do not want to erase, but our concern is for the feelings that lie to us about our intrinsic value and weave their way into our identity.

We are made in the image of God, and so our emotions tell us our Creator has them as well. We have no problem believing the positive emotions of God like joy, love, and hope. But what of the negative ones? In the Bible, we are also told God is an angry and jealous God (Nah. 1:2–6). In fact, there are more references in Scripture to the anger, fury, and wrath of God than there are to his love and tenderness.

How can a good and loving God harbor such emotional vices? We consider wrath as "red-eyed" rage, uncontrollable and destructive. Jealousy is the "green-eyed" monster, envious and resentful. Yet it is not us who calls God these names, but God himself. When he brought the Israelites out of slavery in Egypt, he gave Moses the Ten Commandments, and jealousy was one of the first characteristics he revealed about his nature (Exod. 20:5). He even says his name is "Jealous" (Exod. 34:14). When the people of Israel who are waiting for Moses to come down from the mountain get impatient, build a golden calf, and worship it instead of God, he tells Moses to leave him alone so his wrath can burn against them (Exod. 32:9–10).

Wrath and jealousy are not pretty emotions.

It is important to keep in mind, though, that God's wrath and jealousy are not like ours. When we get angry, it is often a sign of pride and weakness, but God's wrath is his holiness reacting to evil. Our jealousy is a sign of pride and envy, but God's jealousy is born from his zeal to preserve what is precious to him.

Wrath and jealousy are worthy and rightful reactions to injustice and love.

I love my husband and he is precious to me. What if another woman were to flirt with him and try to woo him away from me? I would be angry and jealous. If I were not, it would indicate I do not cherish our relationship very much. God's divine anger and jealousy is a reaction that stems from his love for us. God demands our loyalty because he has that right. Our anger, jealousy, or any feeling that becomes harmful differs from God because our feelings are poisoned by pride.

Some people have trouble reconciling these types of emotions to a God of love. They are all for a God who loves unconditionally but reject a God who is vengeful. But you must understand, God is vengeful because he is loving. You cannot have one without the other. If God is love but is not jealous when we give our heart to something besides him, then his love must not run very deep or true. I had a friend say to me that her God does not hate, to which I responded, "God hates sin." We accept the feel-good emotions of God, but we cannot deny that he is holy and zealous for us. Unlike us, God's wrath is never for the sake of cruelty, his jealousy is never a result of envy, and his hatred is for that which draws us away from him.

Jesus himself had emotions. He cried, showed anger, and was sad. Jesus carried the experience of human feeling with him to his place at the right hand of God and he understands and sympathizes with our feelings, yet he never allowed his feelings to lead him to sin (Heb. 4:15).

No emotion in and of itself is bad. Each is God-given. God says there is a time to weep and laugh, to mourn and dance, to love and hate (Eccl. 3:1–8). There are circumstances where anger is an appropriate response to wrongdoings and injustices. Jesus was genuinely angry at the buying and selling of goods in the sacred temple because ungodly people were making gains in a holy place (Matt. 21:12–13). It is what we do with our emotions that counts. Paul even tells us, "Be angry but do not sin; do not let the sun go down on your anger" (Eph. 4:26).

Anger is not wicked, but we are in trouble if we allow ourselves to remain angry and resort to destructive self-talk. Deal with it promptly. Jesus, through his follower Matthew, says if your friend hurts your feelings, go and tell him (Matt. 18:15–16). He doesn't say go and yell at him or tell him he's an idiot or slam the door—but say, "What you did hurt me, I'm angry about it, and please stop." The friend's reaction is out of your control, but how you handle your feelings in this moment is not.

Quite a few years ago, a coworker accused me of lying. I was not just angry—I was furious. It happened on a Friday, and I let it ruin my entire weekend. I just could not shake the feelings I felt. On Monday morning, I met with my boss and yelled at her for believing the lie that I had lied. One of my coworkers said I was yelling so loud that she could hear me through the closed door.

My over-the-top emotional reaction was inappropriate, and I handled the situation poorly. My feelings drove my actions in the wrong direction.

- The emotion: fear (I feared being perceived as a liar)
- The feeling: anger (my pride was hurt)

- The thought: I must vindicate myself (I needed to set the record straight)

- The action: I lost my temper and yelled (ugly!)

What was the lie I believed? Another person's opinion of me determined my character. I allowed her accusation to make me to feel as if I had to set the record straight and as a result, I was a jerk to my boss, who was caught in the middle.

I began to realize my need to pray a prayer by St. Augustine: "O Lord, deliver me from this lust of always vindicating myself."

In her study *Me Myself and Lies: A Thought Closet Makeover*, Christian author and speaker Jennifer Rothschild reminds us that we have two choices when it comes to our feelings: 1) act according to the truth or 2) act according to the feeling.[51] Feelings must be examined and not automatically deemed valid. They are not to be trusted. The prophet Jeremiah reminds us why we cannot trust our feelings: "The heart is devious above all else; it is perverse—who can understand it?" (Jer. 17:9).

If you think with your feelings, you can fall into all manner of false conclusions. Since our feelings are strong and can hold power over us, we need to run them through the colander of God's wisdom (a.k.a. the truth).

We can find many examples in the Bible of people who acted out of feelings instead of wisdom. Adam and Eve's son Cain murdered his brother Abel. The feeling was jealousy; the result was murder, and the sin was pride (Gen. 4:1–10). King David had an affair with a beautiful woman named Bathsheba. The feeling was sexual longing; the result was adultery and murder, and the sin was lust and lying (2 Sam. 11). The Israelites had God as their King, but they wanted a human king like other nations around them. The feeling was jealousy; the result was arguing with God, and the sin was coveting.

Feelings are not always true, but they are not to be hidden away either. If we leave them unexamined, we never deal with the source and reactions come out sideways. Hard-to-express feelings do not weaken if we keep them bottled up—they grow stronger. When we act from our feelings without wisdom, the results may be catastrophic. We hurt ourselves and others. Hurt people hurt people. Destructive actions can be avoided if we alter what we tell ourselves about our circumstances.

Spiritually speaking, undealt with feelings can occupy two ends of the spiritual spectrum. One is to be overly emotional, and feelings replace faith. The other is to remove feelings from faith altogether, which results in stoicism. Feelings are a part of faith because faith has an experiential element.

Our feelings were meant to be gauges, not guides. They are to report to you, not dictate you. The triggers of negative feelings differ, but the result is usually the same—sinister self-talk. Remember, just because you may feel certain ways—useless, hopeless, unlovable, or worthless—you are not. Do not believe everything you feel.

For Personal or Group Study:

Thoughts to Consider

- What destructive feelings come from your emotions?
- Can you think of a time when you were thinking with your feelings?
- Do your feelings serve you or enslave you?

- What would change in your life if you stopped making choices based on your feelings?
- How have your feelings led to wrongdoing?
- Can you give an example of feelings coming out sideways?
- Can you reconcile the seemingly contradictory idea that God is wrathful and jealous, as well as loving and tender?
- Do your feelings bring about sinister self-talk?

Detect the Lie

- How I am feeling is an indicator of how things really are.
- Emotions are bad, and I should try to suppress them.
- I cannot help it if I have an anger issue.
- Hard-to-express feelings are best left ignored.
- If I can get in touch with my "real" feelings, I will have a better idea of who I am.
- God is angry with me.

Argue against the Lie

- Feelings are not facts.
- Emotions are not bad; what I do with them is what matters.
- I can combat my feelings by relying on God's truth.
- Jesus himself experienced feelings, but never allowed them to lead to sin.
- How I feel fluctuates and is not a determining factor of who I am.
- Sometimes anger is the appropriate response to injustices.
- God hates the sin, not the sinner.

Replace the Lie with the Truth (God's Word)

- "A fool gives full vent to anger, but the wise quietly holds it back" (Prov. 29:11).

- "But the fruit of the Spirit is love, joy, peace, forbearance, kindness, goodness, faithfulness, gentleness and self-control" (Gal. 5:22–23 NIV).

- "A hot-tempered person stirs up conflict, but the one who is patient calms a quarrel" (Prov. 15:18 NIV).

- "Go ahead and be angry. You do well to be angry—but don't use your anger as fuel for revenge. And don't stay angry. Don't go to bed angry. Don't give the Devil that kind of foothold in your life" (Eph. 4:26–27 MSG).

- "For God gave us a spirit not of fear but of power and love and self-control" (1 Tim. 1:7 ESV).

- "One who is slow to anger is better than the mighty, and one whose temper is controlled than one who captures a city" (Prov. 16:32).

- "For we do not have a high priest who is unable to sympathize with our weaknesses, but we have one who in every respect has been tested as we are, yet without sin" (Heb. 4:15).

- "Wrath is cruel, anger is overwhelming, but who can stand before jealousy?" (Prov. 27:4 ESV).

- "For I the Lord your God am a jealous God" (Exod. 20:5).

- "Pride goes before destruction, and a haughty spirit before a fall" (Prov. 16:18 ESV).

CHAPTER 19

"If I were still pleasing people, I would not be a servant of Christ"

(Gal. 1:10).

Hi, my name is Laurie—and I am a people-pleaser.

Ever since I can remember, I have been concerned about what others think of me. Of course, we all have some people-pleasing tendencies. The desire to be liked is universal. The danger comes when we change ourselves to please those around us. We hand over our self-worth and let others shape it for us. Fear of rejection and failure become a constant battle. We lose who we really are, and God made us to be pretty fantastic. Just ask him.

Too many times I sacrificed what I wanted to please someone else because I thought it would make them like me. It did not. And it left me feeling inadequate, stupid, and a little desperate. An article from *Psychology Today* entitled "10 Signs You're a People-Pleaser" hit home. As I read, I was convicted.

1. You pretend to agree with everyone.
2. You feel responsible for how others feel.
3. You apologize often.
4. You feel burdened by all you have to do.
5. You cannot say no.
6. You feel uncomfortable if someone is angry at you.
7. You act like the people around you.
8. You need praise to feel good.
9. You go to great lengths to avoid conflict.
10. You do not admit when your feelings are hurt.[52]

I was also convicted when it was pointed out to me that people-pleasers have trouble saying three simple words: "No, thank you." These words, stated plainly, have no strings attached or emotional baggage hanging off them. A people-pleaser, however, feels the need to explain and apologize for saying no. Say, for example, you have been offered a sandwich. A people-pleasing response may sound like this: "I'm sorry but I am not hungry. I hope that's OK." Or, "Well, if you really want me to have a sandwich then I guess I will."

People-pleasers also have a hard time accepting compliments. If kind words about their efforts, looks, or actions are tossed their way, the tendency is to deflect it. We do not want to be seen as "uppity," and risk offending someone.

It is easy to confuse people-pleasing with kindness. Nobody wants to be perceived as selfish or bad, so we are eager to prove our goodness and likability. This desire to be a good person may allow others to take advantage of us, whether they intend to or not.

Let us look at a fictional person named Marta. She has allowed herself to believe it is her duty to meet the expectations and standards of the people around her. If she does so, she will be liked and therefore happy. She worries about what she wears, says, and does. She does not take criticism constructively but rather views it as a condemnation of her character. Therefore, criticism devastates her. She is a stellar employee, doing everything demanded of her. She is always quick to compliment other people but brushes off any compliment directed at her. If she is told she is wearing a nice dress, she responds dismissively with, "Oh, this old thing? I've had it for years."

Everyone loves Marta, but Marta is miserable. She is always sacrificing her needs and feelings for the sake of others.

It may seem as though sacrificing your needs for others is the right thing to do. After all, the apostle Paul says we are to "regard others as better than yourselves" (Phil. 2:3). And Jesus tells us to love our neighbors as we love ourselves (Mark 12:31). Isn't humility a good trait?

Perhaps a closer look at the definition of humility will help.

C. S. Lewis said, "Humility is not thinking less of yourself; it is thinking of yourself less." Being humble does not mean we put ourselves down, but that we have the right perspective about ourselves and others—we are all sinners, saved by God's grace. We are all God's beloved, which proves we all have great worth. Since our belovedness is unconditional and unearned, we are all in the same boat. One person is not above or below another. It is because of our love for others that we think of their well-being over ours.

Jesus says we are to love others as we love ourselves, not more than ourselves. The problem comes when self-love is lacking and our eagerness to please others stems from our desire to prove we are valuable.

God's love for us hopefully awakens love for ourselves and informs our love for others. We love because God first loved us (1 John 4:19). The apostle John says, "This is how we've come to understand and experience love: Christ sacrificed his life for us. Therefore we ought to live sacrificially for our fellow believers, and not just be out for ourselves" (1 John 3:16 MSG).

As Marta's life progresses, we see her become an angry, bitter person. She begins to believe others perceive her as a doormat. She believes she gives so much of herself, but nobody ever does anything for her. Where is the appreciation for all the sacrifices she has made?

A life of people-pleasing has left her with little self-worth. Her motivation to please people was selfish (she needed to be liked), which led to self-loathing (she sacrificed her needs and feelings for others), which led her to believe she was of no importance to anyone, not even herself.

Does this sound familiar? If so, perhaps it would be helpful to examine the motivation for wanting other people's approval. Do I seek others' approval:

> To feel OK about myself?
>
> To make people owe me?
>
> Because I genuinely love others?
>
> Because I want to make others love themselves as I love myself?

The ultimate question is, "Can I genuinely put another person's interests and feelings before my own and expect nothing in return?"

Of course, there is one person we are to love more than ourselves. Jesus does tell us to love him, trust him, have faith in him, and glorify him. He told us that if we are serious about pleasing God, we are to expect others will dislike us from time to time (Matt. 5:11).

Jesus was not accepted by everyone and still is not. He upset leaders and befriended prostitutes and thieves. These actions did not make him Mr. Popular with the religious folk, who even criticized him for the way he ate (Matt. 9:11). But he was not devastated by what others thought of him, because he kept his eye on his Father and on doing his Father's will. He did not live to please others, but to please his Father in heaven alone.

For most of my life I have fought in the people-pleasing arena, and it has left some scars. I am still in recovery. After a particularly rough relationship, I found I had lost who I was, trying to please the other person. When the relationship fell apart, I had trouble finding the real me. I had been fractured for too long. I had to search for myself, coax her out of the shadows, and put her back together again.

In one of my attempts to reintroduce me to myself, I took a journaling class. The instructor asked us to think of a person we wanted to talk to but were too afraid. Then we were to write him or her letter, knowing it would never be mailed. I chose this person who I had given myself over to.

It was very freeing to write, whine, kvetch, and defend all the feelings I had when it came to our relationship, but the most telling feeling came at the end. I found myself writing repeatedly: "I am lovable. I am lovable. I am lovable." Because the other person had made me—no, scratch that—I allowed myself to believe I was unlovable.

When we try to fit in, we often lose our genuine self. We buy the lie that there are prerequisites to love, acceptance, and worthiness. We change to fit in, which is different than belonging. Brené Brown, in her book *The Gifts of Imperfection,* says, "fitting in and belonging are not the same thing, and, in fact, fitting in gets in the way of belonging. Fitting in is about assessing a situation and becoming who you need to be to be accepted. Belonging, on the other hand doesn't require us to change who we are; it requires us to be who we are."[53]

When I struggle with my self-esteem or worth, the words of my mother often come through to me. When I would agonize in the mirror before a school dance, she would say, "No one's looking at you anyway." She meant that in the nicest way possible, meaning I should quit worrying about what others think because they are all worried about what others are thinking about them. She also told me that if I stopped trying to secure the approval of others, I would draw people to myself because we tend to be attracted to people who are comfortable in their own skin. We are drawn to their inner peace and self-acceptance.

I remind myself that God's opinion of me is the only one that matters. My goal is to be faithful to him in all I do. Some days I nail it; some days I do not. I want to please my Father, not people. I want to please him because I love him, not because I feel as if I must earn his affection or favor.

My mom was a wise lady. And if others do not accept you, what happens? You will discover you can live with it. You will survive. It might not be pleasurable, but it will be tolerable—especially if you remember Jesus's opinion of you is all that matters, and you are the apple of his eye.

For Personal or Group Study:

Thoughts to Consider

- Of the ten signs of being a people-pleaser, did any sound familiar to you?
- How can people-pleasing be confused with kindness?
- How easy or hard is it for you to say, "No"?
- Does criticism devastate you?
- Do you need praise from others to feel good about yourself?
- How do you handle failure?
- Have you ever felt like a doormat?

- How would you define humility?
- When you are kind to someone, do you expect something in return?

Detect the Lie

- The way to be liked by others is to be and do what others want.
- I am a good person if I please other people more than I please myself.
- Other people have the right to judge my actions.
- It is wrong to think my own needs are as important as others' needs.
- Being nice to others guarantees people will be nice to me in return.
- Being what other people want me to be is the best way to be liked.
- If other people do not approve of me, I am a failure.
- If I disagree with someone, they will not like me.

Argue against the Lie

- It is not necessary to be liked by everyone.
- I do not have to earn anyone's approval or acceptance.
- I am a child of God. I am deeply loved by him. I am acceptable to him.
- My needs and wants are as important as other people's.
- I can tolerate rejection. It is not pleasant, but it is not terrible.

- I do not have to have another person's approval to feel good about myself.

- Jesus died on the cross for me, so I can be free from the lie that other people determine my value.

Replace the Lie with the Truth (God's Word)

- "Am I now seeking human approval, or God's approval? Or am I trying to please people? If I were still pleasing people, I would not be a servant of Christ" (Gal. 1:10).

- "There's trouble ahead when you live only for the approval of others, saying what flatters them, doing what indulges them" (Luke 6:26 MSG).

- "We speak as those approved by God to be entrusted with the gospel. We are not trying to please people but God, who tests our hearts" (1 Thess. 2:4).

- "Am I now trying to win the approval of people, or of God? If I were still trying to please men, I would not be a servant of Christ" (Gal. 1:10 NIV).

- "Don't pick on people, jump on their failures, criticize their faults—unless, of course, you want the same treatment. That critical spirit has a way of boomeranging. It's easy to see a smudge on your neighbor's face and be oblivious to the ugly sneer on your own. Do you have the nerve to say, 'Let me wash your face for you,' when your own face is distorted by contempt? It's this whole traveling road-show mentality all over again, playing a holier-than-thou part instead of just living your part. Wipe that ugly sneer off your own face, and you might be fit to offer a washcloth to your neighbor" (Matt. 7:1–5 MSG).

- "And as you wish that others would do to you, do so to them. If you love those who love you, what benefit is that to you? For even sinners love those who love them. And if you do good to those who do good to you, what benefit is that to you? For even sinners do the same. And if you lend to those from whom you expect to receive, what credit is that to you? Even sinners lend to sinners, to get back the same amount. But love your enemies, and do good, and lend, expecting nothing in return, and your reward will be great, and you will be sons of the Most High, for he is kind to the ungrateful and the evil. Be merciful, even as your Father is merciful" (Luke 6:31–36 ESV).

- "You, therefore, have no excuse, you who pass judgment on someone else, for at whatever point you judge another, you are condemning yourself, because you who pass judgment do the same things. Now we know that God's judgment against those who do such things is based on truth. So when you, a mere human being, pass judgment on them and yet do the same things, do you think you will escape God's judgment?" (Rom. 2:1–3 NIV).

- "Live in harmony with one another; do not be haughty, but associate with the lowly; do not claim to be wiser than you are. Do not repay anyone evil for evil, but take thought for what is noble in the sight of all. If it is possible, so far as it depends on you, live peaceably with all." (Rom. 12:16–18 ESV).

- "Here is a simple, rule-of-thumb guide for behavior: Ask yourself what you want people to do for you, then grab the initiative and do it for *them*. Add up God's Law and Prophets and this is what you get" (Matt. 7:12 MSG).

CONCLUSION: CHAPTER 20

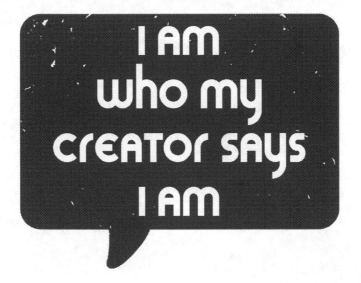

"For this I [Jesus] was born, and for this I came into the world, to testify to the truth. Everyone who belongs to the truth listens to my voice"

(John 18:37).

In California in 1998, Michelle Brown's name and social security number were stolen from a rental application by Heddi Ille. She used Michelle's information from the application to get a driver's license, which she used to drive and to travel extensively. She also used Michelle's identity to buy property and a vehicle worth $32,000, which she failed to pay. Heddi took out a home phone in Michelle's name and did not pay the bill. When Heddi was arrested for trying to smuggle illegal drugs, she used Michelle's name. It took quite some time for Michelle to clear her name. She suffered tremendously because of it. She had to explain that she was not *that* Michelle Brown everywhere she went.

Eventually Heddi was caught and prosecuted for stolen property, but not for identity theft. Even while incarcerated in a federal prison, she was caught sending and receiving mail in Michelle's name, until the real Michelle Brown put a stop to it.[54]

We have a thief among us who is trying to steal our spiritual identity. He makes you feel as though you need to keep paying a debt you do not owe anymore. He accuses you of doing deeds you never did and never lets past failures and regrets rest.

This enemy attempts to blind you to your true identity. Included in his tactics:

- Shame and guilt
- "Stinking thinking"
- Faulty assumptions and presumptions
- Knowing about God without knowing God

- Looking for contentment outside of God
- Worry and anxiety
- The pain of unanswered prayer
- Wallowing in self-pity

This enemy attempts to define you by the world's standards. His strategy is to make you believe the following factors determine your worth:

- You are how you appear.
- You are what you accomplish.
- You are what you acquire.
- You are how you feel.
- You are what other people say you are.

This enemy is real, cunning, and powerful. His weapon of deceit is a two-edged sword. One edge wields the lie that God is not who he says he is. The other edge wields the lie that you are not who God says you are. All your sin and skewed self-worth are a result of believing those lies.

When you combat these lies with the truth, which is God's Word, the abundant life Jesus came to give you is freely yours. You can navigate life's problems and setbacks with joy and grace. God says he is:

- Absolute truth (Num. 23:19)
- All-powerful (Rom. 13:1)
- All-loving (Rom. 8:35, 37–39)
- Ever-present (Ps. 139:7–12)

- Sovereign (Dan. 4:35)
- Holy (1 Pet. 1:15)
- Righteous (Eph. 4:22–24)
- Just (Deut. 32:4)
- Merciful (1 John 1:9)
- Faithful (1 Cor. 10:13)
- Never-changing (Heb. 13:8)

God says you are:

- Beloved and precious (Isa. 43:4)
- His child (Rom. 8:17)
- His friend (John 15:15)
- Justified by Christ (Rom. 3:24)
- A new creation (2 Cor. 5:17)
- Welcomed (Rom. 15:7)
- A temple for God's Spirit (1 Cor. 3:16, 6:19)
- One with Jesus and the Father (John 15:5)
- Blessed (Eph. 1:3)
- Chosen, holy, and beloved (Col. 3:12)
- Redeemed and forgiven (Eph. 1:7)
- God's workmanship (Eph. 2:10)
- Fearfully and wonderfully made (Ps. 139:14)

"God's Spirit touches our spirits and confirms who we really are. We know who he is, and we know who we are: Father and children" (Rom. 8:16 MSG).

The entire Word of God, from Genesis 1:1 to Revelation 22:21, is a love story of God's passionate pursuit of us. God's first question when we were taken by the lie was, "Where are you?" His second question invites us to replace the lie with his truth by answering, "Who told you that?" He immediately set a plan in motion—a plan that brings us back to him. Jesus's final words on the cross, "It is finished," are the completion of that plan (John 19:29).

The Liturgy of Truth

God says to me, "You are mine. I love you. I call you."

I want to believe you Lord. Help my unbelief.

"You are who I, your Creator, says you are. Wholly beloved."

I want to believe you, but I am stubborn.

"Again and again, I declare, 'I know, and I have chosen you.'"

But I feel barren and weary. I feel irrelevant.

"I know, and I have chosen you."

My hands wring. Worry fills my cup.

"I know, and I have chosen you."

I search for contentment outside of your love.

"I know, and I have chosen you."

My heart is fickle. I do not do what I should.

"I know, and I love you still."

I am ashamed. I am too common. A failure.

"Who told you that?"

I have failed. I have allowed a lie to replace your truth.

"Listen, the truth calls to you even now."

I doubt your goodness. I question your will.

"I know the plans I have for you and they are good."

I have not believed you are who you say you are.

"I am who I say I am."

I have not believed I am who you say I am.

"You are my masterpiece. I sing over you. Come home, beloved."

Acknowledgments

I am deeply grateful to many people who have made publishing this book possible.

Doug Neill, my loving and supportive husband. Thank you for the encouragement to pursue my dream and for the patience to listen to my ramblings. You are my rock.

Marianna Malm, my talented and dedicated editor. You made my manuscript clear and concise. I apologize for all the sentences that started with *And* and *But*. The Author Relations representative at the publisher commented that my submitted manuscript was "the best I've ever seen." You made me a better writer. Thank you.

The people who read the various stages of the manuscript and gave helpful and honest feedback. Because so many of you expressed the need for a book like this, I was emboldened to finish it. I owe deepest gratitude to Montana Lattin, Cindy Kopenhafer, Susan Vitalis, Tammy Noteboom, Pr. Corey Bjertness, Pr. Matthew Valan, Alyssa Holmen, and Kate Frappier.

The people of First Lutheran Church, Fargo. Thank you for your prayers and encouragement. I pray you will find life abundant as you locate the lie and replace it with the truth of God.

Endnotes

Prologue

[1] Oswald Chambers, *My Utmost for His Highest: The Golden Book of Oswald Chambers,* edited by James Reimann (Grand Rapids, MI: Discovery House Publishers, 1995), November 30.

Chapter 2

[2] James Martin, SJ, *Seven Last Words: An Invitation to a Deeper Friendship with Jesus* (New York: HarperOne, 2016), 101.

Chapter 3

[3] Chambers, *My Utmost for His Highest,* September 18.

[4] Donald Miller, *Blue Like Jazz: Nonreligious Thoughts on Christian Spirituality* (Nashville: Thomas Nelson, 2008), 8–9.

[5] Bob Sjorgen and Gerald Robison, *Cat & Dog Theology: Rethinking Our Relationship with Our Master* (Colorado Springs: Authentic Media, 2005), 5.

Chapter 4

[6] Timothy Keller, "Talking about Idolatry in a Postmodern Age," Monergism. com, April 1, 2007, https://www.monergism.com/talking-about-idolatry-postmodern-age.

Chapter 5

[7] Stephen R. Covey, *The 7 Habits of Highly Effective People* (New York: Simon & Schuster, 2020), 31.

[8] William D. Backus and Marie Chapian, *Telling Yourself the Truth* (Bloomington, MN: Bethany House Publishers, 2000), 15.

Chapter 6

[9] Barbara Crawford Crafton, "The Geranium Farm," bccrafton@geraniumfarm.
org, June 28, 2018.

Chapter 7

[10] Frank Warren, *PostSecret: Extraordinary Confessions from Ordinary Lives*
(New York: William Morrow, 2005), 2–3.

Chapter 8

[11] Joyce Meyer, *Battlefield of the Mind Devotional: 100 Insights That Will
Change the Way You Think* (Brentwood, TN: Faith Words, 2005), 11.

[12] Remez Sasson, "How Many Thoughts Does Your Mind Think in One
Hour?" SuccessConsciousness, https://www.successconsciousness.com/
blog/inner-peace/how-many-thoughts-does-your-mind-think-in-one-
hour.

[13] "'Derelict' Called Illinois Heiress," *The New York Times*, Feb. 25, 1977,
https://www.nytimes.com/1977/02/25/archives/derelict-called-illinois-
heiress.html.

[14] "7 Bible Verses about God's Wisdom," Knowing Jesus, https://bible.
knowing-jesus.com/topics/God~s-Word-Gives-Wisdom.

Chapter 9

[15] Adelle M. Banks, "Teens Leave Churches Seen as Judgmental, Unfriendly
According to New Book *You Lost Me*," Huff Post, Oct. 9, 2011, https://
www.huffpost.com/entry/teens-leave-churches-seen-as-judgmental-
unfriendly_n_1001528.

[16] Adapted from Carl Medearis, *Speaking of Jesus* (Colorado Springs: David C.
Cook, 2011), 63–69.

[17] "WCK619," "*Orange Is the New Black*—Baptism," YouTube video, posted
Jul. 22, 2013, 1:41, https://www.youtube.com/watch?v=UI0FSuTCAIw.

[18] Timothy Keller, "Christianity does not set itself against thinking .
. ," Twitter, Aug. 28, 2014, https://twitter.com/timkellernyc/
status/504961718024699905.

[19] Rob Bell, *Love Wins: A Book about Heaven, Hell, and the Fate of Every Person
Who Ever Lived* (New York: HarperOne, 2011), 9.

Chapter 10

[20] *The Passion of the Christ.* directed by Mel Gibson (2004, Santa Monica, CA: Icon Productions), Film.

[21] Martin Luther, *A Contemporary Translation of Luther's Small Catechism* (Minneapolis: Augsburg Fortress, 2001), 35.

Chapter 11

[22] David Mathis, "Made for Another World: Remembering C. S. Lewis," Desiring God, November 22, 2016, https://www.desiringgod.org/articles/made-for-another-world.

[23] C.S. Lewis, *The Weight of Glory and Other Addresses* (New York: HarperCollins, 2001), 26.

[24] Timothy J. Keller, "Preparing the Way," Gospel in Life, Jan. 24, 1999, https://gospelinlife.com/downloads/preparing-the-way-6567.

Chapter 12

[25] Don Joseph Goewey, "85 Percent of What We Worry About Never Happens," HuffPost, Aug. 25, 2015, https://www.huffpost.com/entry/85-of-what-we-worry-about_b_8028368.

[26] "Worry," merriam-webster.com, https://www.merriam-webster.com/dictionary/worry

[27] David J. Lose, "Pentecost 5B: Moving from Fear to Faith," davidlose.net, Jun. 19, 2018, https://www.davidlose.net/2018/06/pentecost-5-b-moving-from-fear-to-faith

[28] Chambers, *My Utmost for His Highest,* July 16.

[29] Martin Luther, "A Mighty Fortress Is Our God." Public domain.

Chapter 13

[30] Steve Brown, *Approaching God: Accepting the Invitation to Stand in the Presence of God* (Brentwood, TN: Howard Books, 2012), 72.

[31] Steve Brown, *Three Free Sins: God's Not Mad at You* (Brentwood, TN: Howard Books, 2012), 229.

Chapter 14

[32] "Self-pity," UrbanDictionary.com, https://www.urbandictionary.com/define.php?term=Self-pity&utm_source=search-action.

[33] Lewis B. Smedes, "You can forgive someone almost anything. . .," AZQuotes.com, https://www.azquotes.com/quote/563697, accessed January 04, 2022.

[34] Lewis B. Smedes, "Forgiveness is God's invention for coming . . .," AZQuotes.com, https://www.azquotes.com/quote/523166, accessed January 04, 2022.

[35] Martin, *Seven Last Words*, 26 (italics in original).

Chapter 15

[36] "Dove Real Beauty Sketches," Dove.com, https://www.dove.com/us/en/stories/campaigns/real-beauty-sketches.html

[37] Brands Vietnam, "Dove—Evolution Commercial," YouTube video, posted Mar. 8, 2013, 1:14, https://www.youtube.com/watch?v=KN2yunRynks

Chapter 16

[38] Derek J. Brown, "Martin Luther and the Doctrine of Vocation: A Matter of Discipleship," *Credo*, May 8, 2018, https://credomag.com/article/martin-luther-and-the-doctrine-of-vocation.

[39] Jim Clifton, "The World's Broken Workplace," Gallup.com, June 13, 2017, https://news.gallup.com/opinion/chairman/212045/world-broken-workplace.aspx.

[40] Patrick Lencioni, *The Three Signs of a Miserable Job: A Fable for Managers (and Their Employees)* (San Francisco: Jossey-Bass, 2007), 229–238.

[41] Chambers, *My Utmost for His Highest,* September 2.

[42] C.S. Lewis, *The Complete C.S. Lewis Signature Classics: The Problem of Pain* (New York: HarperCollins, 2007), 577.

Chapter 17

[43] Tony Campolo, *Who Switched the Price Tags?* (Nashville: Thomas Nelson, 1986), 13–14.

44 Barak Goodman and Douglas Rushkoff, *The Persuaders*, https://www.pbs.org/wgbh/pages/frontline/shows/persuaders/etc/script.html.

45 Chris Isidore, "Coke's New Slogan: 'Taste the Feeling,'" CNN Business, Jan. 19, 2016, https://money.cnn.com/2016/01/19/news/companies/new-coke-ad-campaign/index.html.

46 Marlena Telvick, "Charge It!," *Frontline*, https://www.pbs.org/wgbh/pages/frontline/shows/credit/eight/responsibility.html.

47 Bill Fay, "Key Figures behind America's Consumer Debt," Debt.org, May 13, 2021, https://www.debt.org/faqs/americans-in-debt.

48 Lynne Twist, *The Soul of Money: Transforming Your Relationship with Money and Life* (New York: W. W. Norton & Company, 2017), 43–45 (italics in original).

49 "Funny Historical Accounts," http://www.c4vct.com/kym/humor/histor.htm.

Chapter 18

50 Quoted in Donna Soto-Morettini, *The Philosophical Actor: A Practical Meditation for Practicing Theatre Artists* (Chicago: Intellect, 2010), 117.

51 Jennifer Rothschild, *Me, Myself, and Lies: A Thought Closet Makeover* (Nashville: Lifeway Press, 2014), 57.

Chapter 19

52 Amy Morin, "10 Signs You're a People-Pleaser," *Psychology Today*, Aug. 23, 2017, https://www.psychologytoday.com/us/blog/what-mentally-strong-people-dont-do/201708/10-signs-youre-people-pleaser.

53 Brené Brown, *The Gifts of Imperfection: Let Go of Who You Think You're Supposed to Be and Embrace Who You Are* (Center City, MN: Hazelden, 2010), 25.

Conclusion: Chapter 20

54 Grace Ferguson, "Identity Theft: The Michelle Brown Case," Prezi, Feb. 27, 2014, https://prezi.com/koolpb5hwtg4/dentity-theft-the-michelle-brown-case.

Printed in the United States
by Baker & Taylor Publisher Services